Working It Out

GROWING SPIRITUALLY WITH THE POETRY OF GEORGE HERBERT

By Joseph L. Womack

Everyday Education
Making Time for Things That Matter

Everyday Education, LLC

P. O. Box 549

Ashland, Virginia 23005

www.Everyday-Education.com

www.Excellence-in-Literature.com

Front Cover Art: *Cross and Cathedral in the Mountains* by Caspar David Friedrich (1774-1840)

Womack, Joseph L.

Working it out: growing spiritually with the poetry of George Herbert

ISBN: 978-1-61322-034-4

1. Literature—Explication. 2. Literature—History and Criticism. 3. Books and reading. I. Title.

"….continue to work out your salvation…"
Philippians 2:12

To Cynthia,
my light and life

TABLE OF CONTENTS

FOREWORD

Working it Out: Growing Spiritually with the Poetry of George Herbert is a delightful introduction to one of my favorite poets. Although it is written primarily as a devotional, it models a thoughtful method for reading and understanding poetry in general. If you work through it at the pace of one poem a week for a year or so, you will finish the year with a deepened spirituality and a stronger grasp of how poetry works.

Author Joseph L. Womack, a retired college professor, attorney, and Christian minister, presents an orderly method of approaching poetry with an "emphasis on finding and following the movement of thought within the poems." Womack leads the reader through each poem, considering the following elements.

The Big Picture: what the poem is about.

The Parts of the Picture: a stanza-by-stanza explication of the poem with selective identification of literary devices and poetic techniques.

The Parts of the Picture Come Together: an explanation of the movement of thought through the poem.

Reflections: questions for personal meditation.

Scriptures for Further Reflection

To use *Working it Out* as a teaching tool, consider deepening the learning experience by using a modified version of the Model-Based Writing process. Here is how:

- Copy all or part of each poem

- Read it silently; then aloud

- Transform the poem into prose (language in ordinary, non-poetic form)

In your transformation, focus on using strong, vivid words to capture Herbert's meaning. You may wish to take the learning process a step farther and write a poem of your own, based on the form of the poem you are studying. You can learn more about Model-Based Writing at my website, Everyday-Education.com.

To learn more about Herbert and his work, type "Herbert" in the search box at Excellence-in-Literature.com. You will find a longer biography, a few poems, and other resources. I wish you joy in your exploration of the beautiful poetry of George Herbert. May you be blessed and edified during this study.

— Janice Campbell

Everyday Education, LLC, 2014

BIOGRAPHICAL NOTE

George Herbert was born on April 3, 1593, in Montgomery in north Wales, the seventh child in a family distinguished by military and political accomplishments over many years. When he was three, his father died. Though carrying her yet-to-be-born tenth child and overwhelmed by grief and the task that was now hers, his mother Magdalene managed remarkably well. According to one scholar, she was unusually gifted with "grace, intelligence, and literary and musical tastes," and the household was "witty as well as pious."[1] Religion and education she valued highly.

When he was about 12, Herbert's mother enrolled him in Westminster School where his special talents in language and music, already nurtured at home, were developed further. At age 16, he arrived at Trinity College, Cambridge. Already present were two things that would continue with him the rest of his life: writing poetry and suffering ill health. By age 23, he had received two degrees from Cambridge and was appointed an instructor in rhetoric there. Four years later in 1620 he became Public Orator of the University, a position that enabled him to associate with prominent political, literary, and religious figures. His writing of poetry continued (in English, Greek, and Latin), but circulation of his work was considerably restricted. In 1623 and 1624 he served in Parliament, representing his home area of Montgomeryshire.

Although he had been interested in religion for some time, by 1624 his life took a turn toward religious orders. He was ordained a deacon in the Church of England. His path, however, was still uncertain. The years from 1626 to 1629 were full of vocational uncertainty and ill health. It was also a time when many of the poems that were later published in Herbert's major poetic work, *The Temple*, were probably written.

In March 1629 he was wed, thereby beginning a most happy marriage with Jane Danvers. In April 1630, he was installed as rector of the small rural parish of Fuggleston-with-Bemerton near Salisbury and was ordained priest later that year. There he lived the remaining three years of his life in an extraordinary manner. There, in the words of an early biographer, "he lost himself in a humble way."[2] Despite his failing health, he invested his remaining energies fully in vigorous activity: overseeing substantial repair of the church and rectory, taking custody and care of three orphaned nieces, serving his flock ably and humbly, making friends with other priests, writing his classic prose work on being a priest (*A Priest to the Temple*) and composing and revising poems that would be published in *The Temple* after his death.

On March 1, 1633, one month short of his fortieth birthday, Herbert died of consumption. He was buried at Bemerton. According to Izaak Walton (Herbert's most prominent early biographer), before Herbert died he sent a package to his friend, Nicholas Ferrar. It contained Herbert's poetry. Ferrar was to read it and publish it if he thought it would be helpful to others. If he determined otherwise, he was to burn it. Again according to Walton, Herbert described his poetry as containing

> a picture of the many spiritual conflicts that have passed betwixt God and my soul before I could subject mine to the will of Jesus my Master, in whose service I have now found perfect freedom.[3]

By the end of that year, Ferrar had enabled the publication of the first of many editions of Herbert's poems in *The Temple*. Herbert never knew what became of his poetry.

When I claim a place for Herbert among those poets whose work
every lover of English poetry should read and
every student of English poetry should study,
irrespective of religious belief or unbelief,
I am not thinking primarily of the exquisite craftmanship,
the extraordinary metrical virtuosity,
or the verbal felicities,
but of the content of the poems . . .

T. S. Eliot in *George Herbert,* Longmans, Green & Co., 1962.

INTRODUCTION

*I*n doing things Christian, it is often good to begin with confession. I have several. My first confession concerns what I have *not* tried to do in this work. Although most of the scholarly material on George Herbert is rich, brilliant, and useful, and although I have carefully consulted prominent studies of Herbert, this work is not a scholarly effort primarily. Put another way, this work does not attempt to summarize, in any great detail, the historical background of Herbert's time; nor does it attempt to engage, in any significant degree, the vast volume of literary criticism made of Herbert's poetry; nor does it account for the available manuscripts of Herbert's poetry; nor does it focus primarily on literary theory or literary technique and technicalities (although attention is given to techniques used by Herbert within his poems); nor does it attempt to develop a new theory concerning Herbert's poetry or technique. To be sure, all of these things are of enormous importance, and they have received much well-deserved attention by scholars. This work, however, does not follow that path. Instead, it is directed to those who are seeking spiritual guidance and are open to the possibility of finding that guidance in poetry.

The reading of Herbert's poetry has been done mostly by people who are "poetically gifted." Those people are blessed with aptitude and/or training in poetic theory, technique, and technicalities. Thanks be to God for those people, and my hope is that they will find some benefit in this work. But my primary concern is to help expand Herbert's reading audience to people who, though perhaps not "poetically gifted," are open to the experience of poetry in their quest for spiritual guidance. The approach values poetic technique, but the emphasis is on finding and following the movement of thought within the poems.

Herbert's appeal to readers seeking spiritual guidance is inviting, as indicated by these comments about Herbert's role as a "devotional poet":

> George Herbert's collection of poetry, *The Temple*, has a sustained brilliance and an intimacy that makes him the foremost and most influential English devotional poet.[4]
>
> Christopher Hodgkins

> Few (perhaps no) others explored the question of what might constitute 'spiritual life' for a devout Protestant with anything like the sharpness and breadth of vision as [Herbert] did.[5]
>
> Gordon Mursell

> There are only a few extraordinary devotional poets in the [English] language...By any standard George Herbert is the devotional poet proper in English.[6]
>
> Harold Bloom

Since the primary purpose of this work is to assist the reader in connecting with the poetry that has earned Herbert these accolades as a devotional poet, this work is not an end in itself. Like John the Baptist, it points to something much greater than itself. It points to Herbert's poetry, and its sole purpose is to engage the reader with Herbert's poetry. Only that poetry and the reader's experience with it are what really matter.

My second confession is that in offering this work I am asking the reader to do something distinctively un-American. I am asking him to slow down. Reading Herbert is not an experience in fast food; instead, it is more like a multi-course meal of great quality and variety, served in a timely manner and eaten unhurriedly as one savors its delicacy. When asked why he wrote with a pen that required frequent pauses for dipping into an inkwell for a fresh supply of ink, the late Shelby Foote, noted novelist and Civil War writer, answered, "It helps me to slow down." Indeed, there is much good to discover in slowing down. To be sure, slowing down all the time may be asking too much, but asking one to slow down to experience the world of George Herbert's poetry is really asking that person to experience delight.

And there is more. The reading of Herbert's poetry not only calls for the reader's time, it also calls for authentic engagement with, and devotion to, the poetry. Reading Herbert's poetry is somewhat akin to the reading of the Bible as described by Christian spiritualist Eugene Peterson in *Eat This Book*:

> Eating a book takes it all in, assimilating it into the tissues of our lives. Readers become what they read…. If Holy Scripture is to be something other than mere gossip about God, it must be internalized….Words—spoken and listened to, written and read—are intended to do something to us, give health and wholeness, vitality and holiness, wisdom and hope. Yes, eat this book.[7]

But why bother? Why slow down, why take the time, why exert the effort to read Herbert's poetry, and why be devoted to the whole process? In short, why eat Herbert's poetry? The answer is tied to the answer to some other questions, such as:

1. Why, after 375 years since his death, does Herbert's poetry continue to appear in anthologies of English literature?
2. Why is a volume dedicated to his works in *The Classics of Western Spirituality*?
3. Why does he continue to appear in recent prominent fiction and nonfiction works? For example, who is a favorite writer of the well-read preacher/narrator of the Pulitzer Prize winning novel *Gilead*? George Herbert. And who is a prominent poet in the life of Father Tim in Jan Karon's best selling Mitford novels? Herbert. And who is designated as the "poet laureate of prayer" by Philip and Carol Zaleski in their work *Prayer: A History?* Yes, Herbert.

4. And why is Herbert's work listed among the books mentioned by Eugene Peterson as "books that I feel I cannot do without"?[8]

Why, indeed, is this kind of attention given to Herbert?

The answer is that he is a first class poet who, at the same time, speaks profoundly of things Christian. Many voices echo this thought. For example, regarding the quality of Herbert's poetry, the distinguished scholar Joseph Summers in his brilliant study of Herbert describes him as "one of the best English lyric poets."[9] And the prominent English poet Samuel Taylor Coleridge, recognizing the merit of Herbert's poetry, revived interest in Herbert in literary circles in the 19th century. Likewise, T. S. Eliot, one of the most significant English poets of the 20th century, describes Herbert's poetry as "a work of importance for every lover of poetry."[10] The number of admirers goes on and on (see the bibliography for a sampling).

As for the distinctive Christian quality of Herbert's poetry, Richard Baxter, the English Puritan spiritualist of the 17th century, characterized Herbert as "one that really believeth a God and whose business in the world is most with God."[11] Coleridge and Eliot, both Christians, found Herbert noteworthy not only as a poet but also as a Christian. Coleridge summarized his admiration by saying that he found more comfort in Herbert's poetry than that of anyone since John Milton. And Eliot pointed out that Herbert's "poems form a record of spiritual struggle which should touch the feeling, and enlarge the understanding of those readers who hold no religious belief..."[12] Furthermore, Eliot pointed out that the religious contribution of Herbert's poems contained in *The Temple* was greater than that of the work of the more celebrated poet-priest John Donne:

> *The Temple* is ... a record of the spiritual struggles of a man of intellectual power and emotional intensity who gave much toil to perfecting his verses. As such ...I regard it a more important document than all of Donne's religious poems taken together.[13]

This spiritual dimension of Herbert's poetry is the focus of this work. To be sure, the institutional dimension of Herbert's spirituality is important. To say that he valued greatly the Church of England would be an understatement. His deep affection for that Church and its *via media* between the Catholic Church and the Calvinist movement is best expressed in his poem "The British Church." The Eucharist, as administered in the Church of England, often appears in significant ways in his poetry, as do other aspects of *The Book of Common Prayer* of that Church. In addition, his thoughts about being a priest are contained in his classic prose work, *A Priest to the Temple, or the Country Parson*. While noting, however, the importance of the Church in Herbert's life, this volume is primarily concerned with his personal relationship with God, that is, his struggles and successes in "working out his salvation."

In concluding the standard biography of Herbert, Amy Charles states, "No English poet…has represented so fully the relationship between God and man [as did Herbert]."[14] Indeed, it can be argued with good cause that Herbert's primary audience was God rather than the public. First, most of his poems are prayers. Secondly, he seemed not to be interested in publishing his poetry during his lifetime, at least there is no record of his trying to do so in any significant manner. No one seemed to know that he was writing his English poetry. Amy Charles writes that "it appears not even so close a friend as Nicholas Ferrar was aware of the existence of Herbert's English poems until Edmund Duncan was commissioned to carry them to Ferrar shortly before Herbert's death."[15] Herbert left it up to Ferrar to decide whether the poems were worthy of publication. He never knew what Ferrar decided. To be sure, the collection of poetry that Herbert sent to Ferrar was prepared for publication, but Herbert knew that whatever became of his poetry was beyond his control. Publication was obviously an objective, but it was not the reason for the writing of the poetry. As Helen White points out, he wrote to and for God: "…the great thing in the religious experience of Herbert is that he wished to know his God and *for His own sake alone* [emphasis added]…".[16]

The argument that Herbert's writing of poetry was something done for and to God is perhaps best made by himself in his poem "The Quidditie," in which he speaks of his experience with "verse" as an experience with God. "Verse is," he says to God, "that which while I use I am with thee." As Joseph Summers states: "The writing of verse gave to Herbert 'The Quidditie' [or essence] of the spiritual experience."[17]

His writing to and for God and his desire to know his God "for His own sake alone" are reflected in the working out of his relationship with God in his poetry. That relationship was indeed multifaceted and, to some significant degree, it was "Bittersweet," as described in his brief poem bearing that name:

> Ah my dear angry Lord,
> Since thou dost love, yet strike;
> Cast down, yet help afford;
> Sure I will do the like.
> I will complain, yet praise;
> I will bewail, approve:
> And all my sour-sweet days
> I will lament, and love.

Although this poem is certainly not an adequate summary of Herbert's poetry, and although Herbert certainly did not think primarily of God as "angry" (though he certainly acknowledged God's anger), the poem tells much, in broad strokes, about his relationship with God. Because of its brevity, however, the poem is really an enticing tease in that it raises more questions than it answers. In an important sense it is the tip of the iceberg, and as such it is really an invitation to the reader to find out more. And there is much more to be found in the rest of his poems.

And that leads to another confession. Ideally in presenting poems that reflect the working out of a poet's relationship with God, the poems would be arranged in the order in which they were written. Unfortunately Herbert's poems are not dated, and the arrangement of them in *The Temple* is not chronological. The arrangement of the poems in this work, therefore, is governed by another organizing principle. They are presented by topic. For example, the first topic is entitled "Looking Back, Moving Forward." In each of the four poems appearing under this heading the poet reflects upon experiences in his past in light of his present situation, and from this reflection he draws significant spiritual insight about his relationship with God that will enable him to move into the future. This kind of arrangement of the poems is repeated under different topics throughout the work.

Of course, there are inherent limitations to categorizing anything; such limitations are especially apparent when it comes to poetry. The poems are larger and more complex than the topic under which they are categorized. Obviously some poems could be placed in several categories. And hopefully the reader will see the connections between and among the poems that are in different categories. All of this is true, but none of this should diminish the reading experience itself. Indeed, my hope is that this manner of arrangement will enhance the reader's understanding of the general themes reflected in the poet's relationship with God.

The reader, of course, will bring his own sensitivities, experience, interests, and spiritual needs and insights to the reading of these poems. To assist the reader in his reading, I have furnished, first, a general introduction to each topic and the poems presented. Following the presentation of each poem, there are three sections of commentary. The first is entitled "The Big Picture" which provides a general overview of the poem, a way of seeing "the forest" before examining "the trees." It might be good to read this section before reading the poem or right after the first reading of the poem, or both. The next section is entitled "The Parts of the Picture" which is designed to assist the reader in a more detailed and careful reading by breaking the poem into parts and commenting on the development of thought in each part. The third section is entitled "The Parts of the Picture Come Together" which makes an effort to synthesize the parts of the poem. Here the emphasis is on the movement of thought, that is, on how the poem comes together.

After the commentary there is a final section entitled "Reflections." This is for the reader who wants not only to understand and experience the poem but also to spend time reflecting on it in light of the reader's own journey of faith. This section raises some questions that might be helpful in that process. Since this work is most concerned with Herbert's relationship with God and with the spiritual direction that can come from reading his poems, the first two questions for each poem concern this relationship and spiritual direction. There are also references to Scripture that might be of assistance in further reflection. Hopefully these questions and Scripture references will also assist any group that may be reading and discussing Herbert's poetry.

In poetry, the whole is always greater than the sum of the parts. The beauty and truth that a poem contains cannot be reduced to merely an understanding of each of its separate parts or even of how those parts work together. Experiencing fully what a poem has to offer involves experiencing the poem fully in its wholeness. It is my hope and prayer that this work will assist you in experiencing the wholeness of George Herbert's poetry and will thereby enable you to more completely work out your salvation as you come to a better understanding of God's workings in your life.

LOOKING BACK, MOVING FORWARD

*H*erbert's poems are almost always personal in that they capture some personal insight expressed by the speaker in the poem. The following four poems are personal in a special way. In each poem the poet looks back on his life and comes to some significant understanding that will enable him to move forward with greater spiritual insight. *The Glance* provides the big picture of the poet's relationship with God from its beginning to its anticipated heavenly culmination. *The Flower* captures an interval of renewal in which the poet, like a flower in spring, "buds again" as he comes to the realization that "we are but flowers that glide," empowered by God in the upward and downward movements of life. *The Cross* concerns a time of great expectations ending in crushing disappointment. Out of this, the speaker makes a profound spiritual decision. *Affliction (I)* portrays the poet's life in a narrative fashion from the time when God did first entice his heart until the present moment when the poet feels "clean forgot." It is in this moment that the poet comes to a new insight into his relationship with God.

THE GLANCE

When first thy sweet and gracious eye
Vouchsafed even in the midst of youth and night
To look upon me, who before did lie
              Weltering in sin;
    I felt a sugared strange delight,   5
Passing all cordials made by any art,
Bedew, embalm, and overrun my heart,
              And take it in.

Since that time many a bitter storm
My soul hath felt, even able to destroy,   10
Had the malicious and ill-meaning harm
              His swing and sway:
    But still thy sweet original joy,
Sprung from thine eye, did work within my soul,
And surging griefs, when they grew bold, control,   15
              And got the day.

If thy first glance so powerful be,
A mirth but opened and sealed up again;
What wonders shall we feel, when we shall see
              Thy full-eyed love!   20
    When thou shalt look us out of pain,
And one aspect of thine spend in delight
More than a thousand suns disburse in light,
              In heaven above.

The Big Picture

Although brief, the poem spans the time from the beginning of the speaker's relationship with God to its ultimate consummation in heaven. It sparingly but spritely catalogues the delights, the griefs, and the sustaining power inherent in the relationship.

The Parts of the Picture

Stanza 1. The relationship began when God, with "sweet and gracious eye," condescended with favor (or "vouchsafed") to look upon the youthful speaker. The "sweet and gracious" God is contrasted to the speaker "weltering in sin." The effect of this encounter on the speaker is as a "sugared strange delight," greater than the stimulant provided by any cordial or sweet tonic. As a result the speaker's heart is moistened ("bedew"), filled ("embalm"), and taken in as a guest.

Stanza 2. The focus continues on the past, but the imagery changes. Bitter storms emerge with the ability to destroy. But the sustaining power of God's "sweet original joy" worked within the soul of the speaker "and got the day" despite "the surging griefs."

Stanza 3. The poem turns heavenward. The person of focus moves from "I" to "we" The "first glance" of God was powerful (stanza 1) but "sealed up again" (apparently by the grief portrayed in stanza 2). The fulfillment of the relationship will come when we see God's "full-eyed love," and God shall "look us out of pain" in the brilliance of the delight (a return to the imagery of delight in line 5) of "heaven above."

The Parts of the Picture Come Together

As indicated by its title, this poem is about looking – God's looking, in particular. This image holds the poem together (see lines 1, 3, 14, 17, 20, and 21). It is God's looking that begins the relationship with the speaker, and it is God's looking that has sustained the speaker in his grief, and it is God's looking that is the hope for the future.

In the beginning when "first [God's] sweet and gracious eye" looked upon the speaker in his sin, his life became charged with "a sugared strange delight" that brought forth a renewal of heart. As the poem moves forward from this beginning "look," the image emerges of "many a bitter storm" of "surging griefs" in the soul of the speaker. But the "look" which had "sprung from [God's] eye" perseveres as "God's sweet original joy" worked within the speaker's soul, controlled the griefs, and gained the victory.

The first stanza portrays the transforming power of God's "sweet and gracious eye" in the midst of sin. The second stanza reveals God's eye sustaining the speaker's soul in the storms of grief. Then the climax in the final stanza comes with images of "heaven above." There "we shall see [God's] full-eyed love!" There "one aspect" of God will expend delight greater than the light disbursed by a thousand suns. There God shall "look us out of pain."

Reflections

1. What does the poem have to say about relationship with God?
2. What spiritual direction does it provide?
3. If you were writing a poem or other document describing your past experiences with God and your future hopes for your relationship with God, what would you include?
4. The poet chooses the image of God's "looking" to tie together his encounters with God. What image would you choose as the image to tie together your experiences with God?

Scriptures for further reflection:

Deuteronomy 32:9-10
Ezra 5:1-5
Psalms 17:8; 32:8; and 33:18-19
Proverbs 5:21
Hebrews 4:13
Jeremiah 24:6
Revelation 21:1-4; and 22:4-5

THE FLOWER

How fresh, O Lord, how sweet and clean
Are thy returns! even as the flowers in spring;
   To which, besides their own demean,
The late-past frosts tributes of pleasure bring.
          Grief melts away   5
          Like snow in May,
   As if there were no such cold thing.

Who would have thought my shriveled heart
Could have recovered greenness? It was gone
   Quite under ground; as flowers depart   10
To see their mother-root, when they have blown;
          Where they together
          All the hard weather,
   Dead to the world, keep house unknown.

These are thy wonders, Lord of power,   15
Killing and quickening, bringing down to hell
   And up to heaven in an hour;
Making a chiming of a passing-bell.
          We say amiss,
          This or that is: 20
   Thy word is all, if we could spell.

O that I once past changing were,
Fast in thy Paradise, where no flower can wither!
   Many a spring I shoot up fair,
Offering at heaven, growing and groaning thither: 25
          Nor doth my flower
          Want a spring-shower,
   My sins and I joining together.

But while I grow in a straight line,
Still upwards bent, as if heaven were mine own,   30
Thy anger comes, and I decline:
What frost to that? what pole is not the zone,
Where all things burn,
When thou dost turn,
And the least frown of thine is shown?   35

And now in age I bud again,
After so many deaths I live and write;
I once more smell the dew and rain,
And relish versing: O my only light,
It cannot be   40
That I am he
On whom thy tempests fell all night.

These are thy wonders, Lord of love,
To make us see we are but flowers that glide:
Which when we once can find and prove,   45
Thou hast a garden for us, where to bide.
Who would be more,
Swelling through store,
Forfeit their Paradise by their pride.

The Big Picture

This is about renewal—and more! It concerns one spring season in Herbert's life when his "shriveled" heart "recovers greenness," like a flower after returning from "hard weather." The poem is a prayer of praise in which the speaker, while recognizing God's ability to bring a person "down to hell / And up to heaven in an hour," is grateful for this time in which he "buds again." The image of the life cycle of a flower holds the poem together and embodies the message that "we are but flowers that glide."

The Parts of the Picture

Stanza 1. As a prayer of praise, the poem begins with an address of thanksgiving to the Lord for His "returns." The analogy of God's "returns" to the return of flowers in the spring is introduced here and will work its way throughout the poem. As one would expect from the title, the image of the flower in various forms holds the poem together. Lines 3-4 welcome the flowers not only for their own appearance but as a significant sign that frost and winter are past. F.E. Hutchinson is helpful in drawing the theological parallel the speaker intends: "so are the returns of grace the more welcome after a time of spiritual aridity."[18] In response to this renewal of life, grief and snow melt as if they had never been there.

Stanza 2. From the renewal of spring, the focus shifts to a time quite different. It is the time before the renewal, the time of the speaker's "shriveled heart" which he compares to flowers departing downward in winter "to see their mother-root." Lines 12-14 enrich the comparison with the image of the flowers being "dead to the world" in "hard weather" and yet, all the while, able to "keep house unknown" until their present "recovered greenness."

Stanza 3. The focus changes again, this time to the nature of God, addressed as the "Lord of power." As such the Lord is involved in "Killing and quickening, bringing down to hell/And up to heaven in an hour" (surely a reference to emotional states). He is also able to transform "a passing bell" (or one-note of tolling for the mourning for the dead) into a "chiming" of many notes (such as wedding bells or bells calling people to worship). While man speculates "amiss" (or incorrectly) on the meaning of this or that wonder, the speaker points out that "Thy word" (God's revelation) and man could understand if he could "spell" or only learn to read this word.

Stanza 4. After considering (in stanza 3) life's uncertainties and the mutability of all things, the speaker yearns for the immutability of "Paradise" where change and death do not exist. During times of renewal in his past, he has blossomed forth ("I shoot up fair") and offered this beauty or worth to heaven through all the aches and pains of growth ("growing and groaning") – and he has been rewarded or blessed with "a spring shower" even as he and his sins are conjoined.

Stanza 5. This stanza must be taken in tandem with stanza 4. The speaker's growth continues in what he thinks is a straight (or direct and narrow) line upward, but suddenly God's anger is displayed for no apparent reason. Why the anger? It may have appeared for reasons known only to God. On the other hand, there may be a good reason for its appearance. Perhaps it appears in response to the hint of pride overtaking the speaker as he continues upward "as if heaven were mine own." Whatever the reason, God's anger does come and with it the speaker declines. The imagery of winter returns with the reference to "frost." Frost makes flowers decline, but the speaker asks what kind of frost can compare to the power of God's anger? When God turns in this way so that the "least frown" of God is shown, even the extreme cold of the North and South Poles are transformed into "the zone/Where all things burn." Perhaps this is a reference to the burning zone between the tropics of Cancer and Capricorn or perhaps to hell in contrast to the Paradise in line 23.

Stanza 6. In a sudden shift from the previous stanza, the poem reaches its climax in its description of the speaker's renewal. The first two lines of the stanza state the renewal, and the lines that follow provide details. These lines culminate in the speaker's expression of near-disbelief about the transformation he has experienced in his renewal.

Stanza 7. The first line is the same as the first line of stanza 3, except that here God is addressed as "Lord of love" rather than "Lord of power." It is God who uses His wonders and love "To make us see we are but flowers that glide"—an image of ascending and descending that ties together much of the contrasting imagery of the poem. When this truth becomes our own as a result of our experiencing it and finding its truth, then God has a "garden" place (a return to the Paradise imagery of stanza 4) in which we may abide. On the other hand, those who would ignore this truth and strive to be more, "swelling through store" (or being proud through the storing up of possessions), will "Forfeit their Paradise."

The Parts of the Picture Come Together

The movement of thought in this poem is evident in the contrasts of focus found in the stanzas, a focus that (despite the contrasts) always comes back to the Lord's ability to renew. One way to begin understanding this movement is to start near the ending with the opening lines of the final stanza: "These are thy wonders, Lord of love, /To make us see we are but flowers that glide." The phrase "thy wonders" refers to all that has gone before in the poem. In short, all that is recorded in the poem up to this point is "to make us see that we are but flowers that glide." The gliding movement is key, the movement of ascent and descent. The poem is full of both.

It begins with the freshness and cleanness of the "Lord's returns" represented in the flowers of spring. These are "returns of grace." These "returns" melt grief, "like snow in May" as if it never existed. It is a rich image merging the physical (the flowers of spring and snow in May) with the spiritual and emotional (the Lord's "returns" and the passing of grief). The poem, therefore, begins at a high point of the glide, with the uplifting surge of the "Lord's returns" providing the force of the ascending glide.

As the glide continues in the second stanza, a sharp downward movement involving the past is evident. Here are images of a shriveled heart (as opposed to one renewed), "gone/Quite *underground* [emphasis added]; as flowers depart/To see their mother-root." It is a movement in "hard weather" involving an image of death ("Dead to the world") and barely discernible life ("keep house unknown").

Then comes a contrasting uplift of praise (in stanza 3) to the "Lord of power." Both the flowers of the "Lord's returns" in spring and the shriveled heart gone underground are the Lord's "wonders." It is this wondrous power that is the source of the up and down gliding movement and of the extreme emotional conditions of "killing and quickening, the bringing down to hell and the raising up to heaven."

In stanza 4 a specific time is described when the rising movement of the "Lord of power" was most apparent. It is a time replete with upward movement ("I shoot up fair, /Offering at heaven") and yearning for "Paradise, where no flower can wither!" At the peak of the upward movement (lines 29-30), the descent begins again (as in stanza 2). The cause of "decline" is abundantly clear—God's anger. It is this anger, this "frown" of God, that can turn the poles of extreme cold to "the zone/Where all things burn," the opposite of Paradise.

As the poem moves to its climax (stanza 6), it is again God's power ("my only light") that propels the movement upward. Life returns to the speaker as, like the flowers, he "buds again," living and writing, smelling the dew and rain, and relishing his writing. It is a picture of fully abundant life with no place for the past tempests of the night. As the speaker concludes, he addresses God as the "Lord of love." The flight ends on this note of love. It is a flight that brings the message that "we are but flowers that glide." In short, our lives resemble a gliding motion of ascending and descending that is empowered by God who reveals Himself as both "Lord of power" and "Lord of love." This message is key to the finding of peace that passes understanding; for once we find and prove the truth of this message, we find our garden, our place "to bide" (an allusion to Jesus' call for us to abide in him?).

Surely this may refer to the Paradise of heaven, but this poem is about the gliding movement of life on this earth. Taken within that context, the message of line 44 is about life in this world. It is a message about our finding a peace that passes understanding as we experience the Lord of power and of love in the up's and down's of life. It is a message about our working out our salvation, as God works in us to will and to work for His good pleasure (Philippians 2:12-13). In contrast, the last lines of the poem issue an admonition or warning to those people who live on the basis of their pride, the "swelling" or attempting to ascend with possessions and not with God's power. These people "forfeit" this place of Paradise that is available to those who come to know that "we are but flowers that glide," empowered by the Lord of power and, most of all, by the Lord of love.

Reflections

1. What does this poem have to say about relationship with God?
2. What spiritual direction does it provide?
3. How do you react to the statement in the poem that "we are but flowers that glide"? On the basis of what is said in the poem, do you think this means that our lives resemble a gliding motion of ascending and descending that is empow-

ered by God who reveals Himself as both "Lord of power" and "Lord of love"? How do you respond to that idea? Or do you think the statement means something else?

4. This poem is driven by a time of renewal in the speaker's life. From this experience, he draws conclusions about the ways in which God has worked in his life. What has been your experience with times of renewal in your life? How and when have they come, and how do you see God at work in them?

5. What about the movements downward in your life? Consider the image in the second stanza of the flowers in winter departing downward to "see their mother-root," where "dead to the world," they "keep house unknown." How is this image of withdrawal (in a time of "hard weather") to something foundational and sustaining potentially comforting for one who is experiencing a downward movement in life?

Scriptures for further reflection:

Psalms 51:10
Psalms 103:1-5
Ecclesiastes 3:1-8
Isaiah 40:29-31
Lamentations 5:21
Romans 8:37-39

THE CROSS

What is this strange and uncouth thing?
To make me sigh, and seek, and faint, and die,
Until I had some place, where I might sing,
     And serve thee; and not only I,
But all my wealth and family might combine   5
To set thy honour up, as our design.

And then when after much delay,
Much wrestling, many a combat, this dear end,
So much desired, is given, to take away
     My power to serve thee: to unbend   10
All my abilities, my designs confound,
And lay my threatenings bleeding on the ground.

One ague dwelleth in my bones,
Another in my soul (the memory
What I would do for thee, if once my groans   15
     Could be allowed for harmony):
I am in all a weak disabled thing,
Save in the sight thereof, where strength doth sting.

Besides, things sort not to my will,
Even when my will doth study thy renown: 20
Thou turnest the edge of all things on me still,
     Taking me up to throw me down:
So that, even when my hopes seem to be sped,
I am to grief alive, to them as dead.

To have my aim, and yet to be   25
Further from it than when I bent my bow;
To make my hopes my torture, and the fee
     Of all my woes another woe,
Is in the midst of delicates to need,
And even in Paradise to be a weed.   30

Ah my dear Father, ease my smart!
These contrarieties crush me: these cross actions
Do wind a rope about, and cut my heart:
      And yet since these thy contradictions
Are properly a cross felt by thy Son,   35
With but four words, my words, Thy will be done.

The Big Picture

This poem was written at a time when Herbert had received a position in a church which some scholars say was the church at Bemerton where he was serving at his death. However, Amy Charles, the most prominent of Herbert's biographers, says the church was at Leighton Bromswold and the time 1626, four years before his becoming rector at Bemerton.[22] Soon after coming to this church in the leadership role of deacon, he became ill and was unable to fulfill his hopes of doing the Lord's work in the way he had planned. The poem is a prayer filled mostly with his frustrations about those unfulfilled hopes and plans. He wants to know how God is at work in all this. In working through this situation, the speaker considers the Cross, and there everything changes.

The Parts of the Picture

Stanzas 1-3. These stanzas make clear the nature of this "strange and uncouth thing" that burdens the speaker with disappointment and bewilderment as he opens the poem. The first stanza describes the anticipation leading up to the speaker's having "some place" where he could sing and serve God and to which his wealth and family also could be committed to the endeavor of honoring God. Much sighing, seeking, fainting, and dying had preceded the finding of "this place." Then, after the "delay, wrestling, and combat," the "dear end" of having a "much desired" church is given—but then taken away. This giving and taking eliminates his power to serve God, "unbends" (or weakens) his abilities. "confounds" his plans, and scatters the life-giving blood of his "threatnings" (or intentions). Stanza 3 provides more details. An "ague" (or disease) now dwells in his flesh, and another dwells in his soul. This latter one is the memory of what he desired to do for God if only "harmony" (or some sense of balance) had come to his "groans" or woes. He summarizes his situation in lines 17-18 by describing himself as "a weak disabled thing," except that to see his outward appearance ("the sight thereof") does not reveal his weakness but suggests strength. That discrepancy causes "sting" or pain.

Stanza 4. The focus now shifts. Up to this point, the speaker has been addressing God (as indicated by the "thee's" in lines 4, 10, and 15), and while speaking to God, the speaker has been thoroughly enmeshed in describing his woes. With stanza 4, there is a pronounced change in tone as the speaker becomes more confrontational, more involved in a quarrel with God. Now the poem shifts more to the cause of this situation rather than merely describing the situation. Things do not turn out in accord with the speaker's will even when his will "doth study" God's "renown." Lines 21 and 22 become more intense with direct, unqualified accusations that God turns all things on him and takes him up only to cast him down. And even when his hopes "seem to be sped," he is dead to them and alive only to grief.

Stanza 5. The speaker turns away from his direct confrontation with God and begins to summarize his plight. He is like one who has taken aim with his bow but then finds himself farther from his target than when he first took aim. His failed hopes have turned into torture. It is as if he has to pay a fee for his woes, and the fee is yet another woe. The culminating comparison comes in lines 29 and 30. His condition makes him like one who is in the midst of "delicates" or delights (as he is with having found a place to serve God) but also finds himself in need (as he does because he has had the power to serve taken away from him). It is as if he were a weed in Paradise.

Stanza 6. The speaker turns again to address God directly. But now the bitterness of stanza 4 is gone. Now the address is tender: "Ah my dear Father." And the request is for relief: "ease my smart!" He speaks again of his state of being: "the contrarieties crush" him, and the "cross actions" cut his heart. All of this leads him to thoughts of the Cross and the "contradictions" felt by Christ. With this, the speaker submits to God's will as he claims the words of Jesus at Gethsemane.

The Parts of the Picture Come Together

Expectations, hopes, dreams are so very important. They sustain us, energize and otherwise empower us, guide us, nurture our spirit, and fulfill our need for purpose. Then, after much striving, for one to see these dreams "given" (or realized) only to see them "taken away" almost at the same time—all this leads to despair. It is at this point of despair (and for those reasons) that this poem begins.

Despair is encapsulated in the question in the opening line. The question concerns the "what is" or the nature of the situation. For three stanzas, the nature of this situation is described. First, there are the expectations, all centered in the speaker's desires. In two lines (3 and 4), "I" is used three times. To be sure, all of this self-centeredness is with the best of intentions—to "serve thee" (repeated in line 10) and "To set thy honour up." But for whatever motivation that there is to serve God, the speaker is wrapped up primarily in the expectations of his own will.

An elaboration of the details of his will and of the depth of his disappointment pours forth in stanzas 2 and 3. Certainly his despair is understandable, and his disappointment is deep for good cause, but dwelling on self becomes more elaborate as the details unfold. For example, in the three lines that conclude stanza 2, "my" occurs four times, and in the three opening lines in the next stanza, "my" and "I" are used four more times. His case before God has been presented. Indeed, he is a "weak disabled thing," and, one might add, he is totally self-absorbed in his loss.

Having spent the first half of the poem on describing his condition to God, the speaker now directly confronts God. Stanza 4 begins with a pronounced understatement: "things sort not to my will," even when his will is focused on God. Simply stated, the speaker has done his part with his will, but apparently God has lapsed in doing His part. That lapse is frankly and bitterly described in lines 21-22. The litany of woes continues in the remainder of stanza 4 and in all of stanza 5, as does the self-absorption. Note the use of "my" and "I" five times in the opening four lines of stanza 5, repeating the pattern of the closing half of stanzas 1 and 2, the opening half of stanza 3, and the closing half of stanza 4. He sums up his state with the poignant image of one standing in need while surrounded by delights, like a weed in Paradise.

Although the final stanza begins with the focus on self (note the three "my's" and the "me" in the first three lines) that characterizes the preceding stanzas, everything begins to change. It is as if the speaker begins to reap the benefits of having expressed himself fully to God in the previous stanzas. He has had his time before God; he has had his say to God. He has had his time of "take this cup from me." He needed that. Now a kind of peace begins to emerge, as reflected in the opening words of the final stanza: "Ah my dear Father." Here is reconciliation beginning to happen with relationship being restored and bitterness receding. The nature of his request reflects all this: "ease my smart!" He does not forget his condition. Indeed, a stark description of his state is given: the "contrarieties crush" him as "these cross actions" cut his heart. But the rebellion is gone—as is the self-absorption! Now the thought of "cross actions" leads him out of himself to the Cross of Christ and to all the "contradictions" felt by Him on the Cross. At this moment of diminished self and heightened Christ, the speaker claims the words of Christ "Thy will be done." What has started as the worst of defeats for the speaker has ended in the victory of submission.

Reflections

1. What does this poem have to say about relationship with God?

2. What spiritual direction does it provide?

3. How do you respond to the speaker's reaction to his situation and to God in the first 5 stanzas? Is it wise to talk to God with such depth of honest feelings? Could this approach be seen as a kind of healthy therapy that is useful at times in the process of restoring a right relationship with God? Or is this reaction too laden with self-pity?

4. What has been your experience with your own failed expectations and hopes that developed and then vanished or never really developed? How do you deal with the issue of God being at work in that kind of experience?

5 Does the poem offer any assistance to you in responding to the ways of God when you find yourself in a situation where all you can do is ask (as the poet does in the first line of this poem) "What is going on here?"

6. Is the poem helpful to you in assisting someone else in a situation where that person wants to understand a bewildering situation and wants to find out how God is or has been at work in it?

7. Is simply saying "Thy will be done" sometimes (or always?) the best answer to a situation we cannot understand?

Scriptures for further reflection:

Psalms 22
Habakkuk 1:1-4 and 3:17-19
Mark 14:32-42
II Corinthians 12:8-10

AFFLICTION (I)

When first thou did entice to thee my heart,
                    I thought the service brave:
So many joys I wrote down for my part,
                    Besides what I might have
Out of my stock of natural delights,   5
Augmented with thy gracious benefits.

I looked on thy furniture so fine,
                    And made it fine to me:
Thy glorious household-stuff did me entwine,
                    And 'tice me unto thee.   10
Such stars I counted mine: both heaven and earth
Paid me my wages in a world of mirth.

What pleasures could I want, whose King I served,
                    Where joys my fellows were?
Thus argued into hopes, my thoughts reserved   15
                    No place for grief or fear.
Therefore my sudden soul caught at the place,
And made her youth and fierceness seek thy face.

At first thou gavest me milk and sweetnesses;
                    I had my wish and way: 20
My days were strewn with flowers and happiness;
                    There was no month but May.
But with my years sorrow did twist and grow,
And made a party unawares for woe.

My flesh began unto my soul in pain,   25
                    Sicknesses cleave my bones;
Consuming agues dwell in every vein,
                    And turn my breath to groans.
Sorrow was all my soul; I scarce believed,
Till grief did tell me roundly, that I lived.   30

When I got health, thou tookest away my life,
                              And more; for my friends die:
My mirth and edge was lost; a blunted knife
                              Was of more use than I.
Thus thin and lean without a fence or friend,   35
I was blown through with every storm and wind.

Whereas my birth and spirit rather took
                              The way that takes the town;
Thou didst betray me to a lingering book,
                              And wrap me in a gown.   40
I was entangled in the world of strife,
Before I had the power to change my life.

Yet, for I threatened oft the siege to raise,
                              Not simpering all mine age,
Thou often didst with academic praise   45
                              Melt and dissolve my rage.
I took thy sweetened pill, till I came where
I could not go away, nor persevere.

Yet lest perchance I should too happy be
                              In my unhappiness,   50
Turning my purge to food, thou throwest me
                              Into more sicknesses.
Thus doth thy power cross-bias me, not making
Thine own gift good, yet me from my ways taking.

Now I am here, what thou wilt do with me   55
                              None of my books will show:
I read, and sigh, and wish I were a tree;
                              For sure then I should grow
To fruit or shade: at least some bird would trust
Her household to me, and I should be just.   60

Yet, though thou troublest me, I must be meek;

<blockquote>In weakness must be stout.</blockquote>

Well, I will change the service, and go seek

<blockquote>Some other master out.</blockquote>

Ah, my dear God! Though I am clean forgot,   65

Let me not love thee, if I love thee not.

The Big Picture

This is a "journey" poem portraying numerous feelings arranged in a narrative manner around the development of the poet's life. It is difficult to define and date all the events, but it is clear that the poem tracks the poet's relationship with God from its beginning, through his conflicting desires and emotions along the way, and finally to the crisis of faith out of which he writes. A good way to approach the poem initially is simply to listen to the story.

The Parts of the Picture

Stanzas 1-4. Here is a catalogue of the delights of the poet's heart joining to God through "service brave," "many joys," "natural delights," and "gracious benefits." Here is oneness with God's natural wonders of creation (stanza 2) and the joy of service and seeking God with no thought of grief (stanza 3). Here is the pleasure of having his "wish and way" (stanza 4). Then the poem turns.

Stanza 5-9. "My flesh began my soul to pain" (line 25) announces the deterioration of body and spirit that runs through these stanzas. Note the stark contrast with the first part of the poem. There is physical deterioration (stanza 5). There is social isolation with the death of friends (which probably includes family). There are feelings of being as useless as a "blunted knife" and of being without "a fence [protection] or friend" (stanza 6). With stanza 7, "the way that takes the town" emerges. This is a new kind of estrangement—the tempting deception of worldly success. It comes in the form of academic achievement: "a lingering book" (line 39), "a gown" (line 40), and "Academic praise" (line 45). Finally he finds himself paralyzed, unable to "go away, nor persevere." With stanza 9, there is more sickness and a bitter declaration, in lines 53-54, that God has changed the poet's direction ("Thus doth thy power cross-bias me") and thereby has taken from him his ways and prevented his gifts from developing.

Stanzas 10-11. What will God do now? The poet's books do not have the answer. At the nadir of the hopelessness that comes from self-pity, he wishes to be a tree and at least benefit a bird (lines 57-60). Lines 61-62 speak of his need to be both "meek" and "stout" in the midst of God's troubling him. In the next two lines the poet threatens to leave God and "seek some other master out." In line 65 the poem begins to resolve itself with an address to "my dear God" who has "clean forgot" the poet. The concluding line is a petition, a desire for a higher form of love of God, a plea to be empowered to love God completely or not at all.

Rhyme Scheme: Always precise in forming his stanzas, Herbert uses his rhyme scheme effectively here. He connects the first four lines of each stanza with an interlocking rhyme (such as *abab* in the first stanza) and usually uses them to present a unit of thought. Then he ends each stanza with a rhyming couplet (*cc*) which he often uses to summarize (lines 11-12, 17-18, 29-30, 35-36, 41-42, 47-48, and 53-54) or make a transition (lines 23-24) or conclude (65-66).

Vocabulary:

   a. line 2, brave: splendid

   b. line 7, furniture: the natural world of God's creation.

   c. line 13, want: lack

   d. line 21, strawed: covered as with straw

   e. line 44, simpering: smirking

The Parts of the Picture Come Together

The movement of the poem follows the narrative of the poet's spiritual journey. As John Wall points out, the poem is "about a speaker who has increasing difficulty in understanding the narrative of his life in terms of God's actions."[25] The narrative has a beginning, middle, and end.

The beginning is found in the first four stanzas which portray the bliss of the poet's coming to God and the joy of his first stage of relationship with God. As Coburn Freer so aptly indicates, these stanzas "move gracefully and elegantly."[26] Here is the "honeymoon" of the speaker's relationship with God when "there was no month but May" as the speaker had his "wish and way." With the last two lines of stanza 4, the transition to the middle stage begins.

Stanzas 5-9 give a picture of increasing despair. Consider the change in language about God's actions in the poet's life. In the first four stanzas, God did entice, "did me entwine," and "gavest me milk and sweetness." In stanzas 5 through 9, God "tookest away my life," "did betray me," "did...melt and dissolve my rage," "throwest me into more sickness," and "doth... cross-bias me." God has undergone a complete reversal of roles, or so it seems to the poet.

In the final two stanzas, the current stage of the speaker's relationship with God is considered as he ponders what God will do. The answer is not to be found in books—or elsewhere. The speaker is, therefore, pressed with another question: What is he to do? Then comes the climactic last stanza where the conflicts of the poem are intensely compacted and then resolved in a powerful paradox. The resolution comes to a climax in the last two lines. Though the poet feels "clean forgot" by God, he calls out to God. It is a petition ("let") for God to allow the poet to love God unconditionally or not at all. As F. E. Hutchinson says, if the poet "cannot hold onto his love of God even when he feels forsaken or unrewarded, he had better not hope to love at all."[27]

The poet has come to an understanding, not from his books but from the experience of his journey. It is not an understanding of God's ways but of the poet's need to love God no matter what His ways are. The poet's journey has led him to a piece of the bedrock of Christian spirituality, as described by John Wall: "What the speaker performs at the end of this poem is letting God be God."[28]

Reflections

1. What does the poem have to say about relationship with God?
2. What spiritual direction does it offer?
3. Of what value is there in listening to the stories of others?
4. How do you respond to the different stages in the development of the poet's relationship with God?
5. What value is there in looking at the story of your relationship with God? How would you describe the different stages in your journey with God?

Scriptures for further reflection:

Ruth 1:21
Psalms 9:18; 10:17; 25:16-17; 31:10; 71:20-21; 73:26; and 77:4-12
Matthew 11:28-30
Romans 12:12

LETTING GO

*E*ach of these poems deals with a different aspect of "letting go" to God. *The Holdfast* portrays the process or the stages the speaker goes through until he finds the true holdfast in Christ alone. *Submission* is a delightful exploration of an alternative to letting go. *Obedience* uses the method of a legal conveyance through a written document to describe the speaker's surrender to God with an invitation to others to do likewise.

THE HOLDFAST

I threatened to observe the strict decree
    Of my dear God with all my power and might.
    But I was told by one, it could not be;
Yet I might trust in God to be my light.
Then will I trust, said I, in him alone.   5
    Nay, even to trust in him, was also his:
    We must confess that nothing is our own.
Then I confess that he my succour is:
But to have nought is ours, not to confess
    That we have nought. I stood amazed at this,   10
    Much troubled, till I heard a friend express
That all things were more ours by being his.
    What Adam had, and forfeited for all,
    Christ keepeth now, who cannot fail or fall.

The Big Picture

In "letting go" to God, the speaker moves through several stages: from one who is confident in his ability to "observe the strict decree," to one who realizes that he cannot trust on his own since even trusting is a gift from God, and finally to one who finds true security is knowing that all things rest in Christ and thereby are "more ours by being his."

The Parts of the Picture

Possible Biblical Allusions in the Title. See Hebrews 4:14-16; Psalm 73:28; and I Thessalonians 5:21.[29]

The Personae. At least two people are at work in this poem. The speaker is primary, but there is at least one other person referred to as "one" in line 3 and as "a friend" in line 11. These may or may not be the same person. In fact, the interplay between the speaker and another person holding another point of view runs throughout the poem. In lines 1-2, the speaker declares; in lines 3-4 the "one" tells him otherwise. In line 5, the speaker declares again; in lines 6 and 7, his declaration is again found faulty. In line 8, the speaker restates his corrected position, only to have it corrected again in lines 9-10a. In lines 10b -11, the speaker states his amazement and troubled state, only to have "a friend" provide lasting assurance in line 12. The speaker then is able to provide, without refutation, the concluding couplet. Thus, it is through the prodding of someone else with a differing point of view that the speaker is moved through the steady process of letting go to God, of finding the true "holdfast."

Lines 1- 4. The poem opens with a threat that has a somewhat comic undertone, especially when considered in light of the development of the poem. The speaker "threatens" with all his "power and might" to "observe the strict decree." This vow of obedience based on self-sufficiency is the starting point. The "But" of line 3, however, turns the poem in another direction. The advice of "one" (an advisor and/or the "friend" of line 11) is that such strict observance "could not be." Yet there is an alternative: trust.

Lines 5-8. The speaker takes this alternative: "Then will I trust in him alone." But this is not enough. Even trusting is God's. Lines 7 and 8 provide another possibility: the humble confession that "nothing is our own." So the speaker confesses that only God is his sustaining power. Surely this is enough.

Lines 9-12. But this is not enough either. There is yet another letting go. Confession is not enough for such confession is not ours. Only "nought" is ours. This realization leaves the speaker "amazed" and "much troubled." Then "a friend" expresses the central truth of the poem in the irony of line 12. The speaker finds ultimate security in all things belonging to God. Hence, all things are "more ours by being his" since only in God do things endure.

Lines 13-14. The concluding couplet restates this truth: all that was lost beginning with Adam's sin is now eternally secure in Christ.

The Parts of the Picture Come Together

Letting go to God is a process, or so it is in this poem. The title is not mentioned in the poem (a common occurrence for Herbert), but it does provide a clue to understanding the process that occurs in the poem. The speaker "holds fast" to several points of view until he finds the true "holdfast." Indeed, the movement of thought follows these different points of view. First, there is the bluster of self-sufficiency, a declaration by the speaker to act in obedience to the strict law. This is the apex of the speaker's self-confidence in his own works. It is a statement brimming with boldness, self-assurance, commitment, and even devotion ("my dear God"). To this threat, the speaker "holds fast." What more could God ask? But, as the rest of the poem shows, God wants something radically different.

"One" tells the speaker that his vaunted pride of self-sufficiency will not do. Perhaps the speaker "might trust" in God rather than rely on his "power and might." It is to trust, then, that the speaker "holds fast." He will trust—but the speaker comes up short again. He is still in "his will." He has let go of his "power and might" but still is centered in his ability to act and is thereby still deficient. Trust is a gift from God, not a source of self-redemption.

And so the speaker turns to confession. To this he will "hold fast." But even the self's claim on confession must go, even the confession that "nothing is our own." Everything is to go—until we know "we have nought." That's when the amazement and trouble of the grace experience occurs. To what is there to "hold fast"? The bottom has been reached, at which point the clarity of the highest truth appears: "all things are more ours by being his." Here is the final "holdfast" as the speaker finds true security is realizing that all is in God. This is security that transcends all of man's "power and might" and extends beyond his finiteness. All is found in God when all of self is lost. The process culminates in our nought and in God's everything. As Saint Augustine put it, "We are restless, O Lord, until we find our rest in Thee."

The process of letting go to God, of finding the true "holdfast," is culminated in what "Christ keepeth." Christ is the ultimate "holdfast." And that is cause for the celebration of the closing couplet. As Richard Strier points out, "'The Holdfast' does not pose a dilemma. It celebrates a—the solution…. Praise … is the final word."[30]

Reflections

1. What does this poem have to say about relationship with God?
2. What spiritual direction does it provide?
3. How do you respond to the process that the speaker goes through before he finally discovers that "we have nought" and that "all things were more ours by being his [God's]"? What does "all things are more ours by being God's" mean to you?
4. To what do you "hold fast"? Or put another way, in what do you find ultimate security? It is easy to say "God," but how do you know you mean it? Does the living of your life reflect God as your "holdfast"—some of the time, all of the time, or none of the time?

Scriptures for further reflection:

Ephesians 2:8-9
Philippians 3:4-9
Colossians 1:15-20

SUBMISSION

But that thou art my wisdom, Lord,
    And both mine eyes are thine,
My mind would be extremely stirred
    For missing my design.

Were it not better to bestow   5
    Some place and power on me?
Then should thy praises with me grow,
    And share in my degree.

But when I thus dispute and grieve,
    I do resume my sight,   10
And pilfering what I once did give,
    Disseize thee of thy right.

How know I, if thou shouldst me raise,
    That I should then raise thee?
Perhaps great places and thy praise   15
    Do not so well agree.

Wherefore unto my gift I stand;
    I will no more advise:
Only do thou lend me a hand,
    Since thou hast both mine eyes.   20

The Big Picture

    This poem deals with a serious subject in a delightful manner. After the speaker acknowledges the benefits of submission to God, he then considers an alternative. He suggests that maybe it would be better if the Lord bestowed "Some place and power" on him. After considering what would probably happen if the Lord did that, the speaker returns to a state of submission with a closing plea for the Lord to "lend me a hand."

The Parts of the Picture

Outline. The beginning, middle, and end are clearly evident. The first stanza states the speaker's submission to the Lord; stanzas 2-4 are concerned about the possibility, and the probable consequences, of the Lord's giving him "place and power"; and, in stanza 5 the speaker returns to a submissive state.

Stanza 1. This is a statement to the Lord of the speaker's submissive state and its benefits. He is dependent on the Lord's being his wisdom and eyes. If that were not the case, he would be "missing my design" or being out of God's will for his life. This is his condition, but with the next stanza, his "wisdom" and "eyes" begin to wander.

Stanzas 2- 4. The questioning (and subdued humor) begin with stanza 2: would it not be better, the speaker asks, if the Lord gave him "some place and power"? If that were the case, surely praises to the Lord would grow, also. Coburn Freer's summary of the speaker's statement is a good one: "Make me powerful and rich and You too will look good."[31] With stanza 3, the speaker begins to question his reasoning. He realizes that this disputing with the Lord means that he is "resuming my sight" or taking back his eyes that he has given the Lord (as indicated in line 2). This "pilfering" would "disseize" (or sever) from God His "right" to what the speaker has. In stanza 4, the speaker's wayward desire for "place and power" comes to a climax as the folly of his desire to be elevated is exposed. After questioning whether he would raise God if God should raise him, he realizes, in a subtle understatement, that "Perhaps" being in great places and praising God "Do not so well agree."

Stanza 5. Having completed his consideration of being elevated to a place of power, the speaker returns to submission. He recommits the gift of himself that he has made to the Lord and "will no more advise." He cannot close, however, without some light-hearted seriousness as he reminds the Lord to "lend me a hand" since the Lord has "both mine eyes" (a repetition of the phrase used in line 2).

The Parts of the Picture Come Together

Notice how the poem makes its case for submission. First, the speaker attributes his not missing his "design" to his submission; that is, his wisdom and eyes are tied to the Lord and thereby he has found God's purpose for himself. Here is a concise statement of the condition of submission (wisdom and sight tied to the Lord) and of its benefits (it's the way to finding one's "design").

The next step is to consider an alternative. The speaker playfully considers the possibility of possessing "place and power." Would it not be "better" (than submission, we assume) if God gave the speaker this kind of prestige? In effect, the poem makes its case for submission by considering something possibly better, that is, "place and power." But as the consideration of this way of power proceeds, it crumbles in on itself. The disadvantages become readily apparent. Going in that direction means taking back what the speaker has already given God and probably involves a forgetting of God since great places and praise of God do not usually go together. In short, the speaker has openly explored a possibly better way than submission and found it significantly lacking.

Finally, therefore, there is a return to submission—but not without a reminder to the Lord that the speaker is in need of a helping hand! Delightfully, playfully, with subtle humor, the speaker has made the case for submission. Its benefits are considerable; the alternative is fraught with undesirable side effects. Submission is the place to be—as long as the Lord lends a hand!

Reflections

1. What does the poem have to say about relationship with God?
2. What spiritual direction does it provide?
3. How would you characterize submission to God? How does one achieve it? Or does one achieve it? Is obtaining this kind of submission more of a gift from God than an achievement of one's self? Or is it both?
4. What are the difficulties of submission to God? What are impediments to achieving it? What are its benefits?
5. The poem considers one alternative to submission—"place and power." Are there other alternatives?

Scriptures for further reflection:

Luke 15:11-24

OBEDIENCE

My God, if writings may
Convey a Lordship any way
Whither the buyer and the seller please;
    Let it not thee displease,
If this poor paper do as much as they.   5

    On it my heart doth bleed
As many lines, as there doth need
To pass itself and all it hath to thee.
    To which I do agree,
And here present it as my special Deed.   10

    If that hereafter Pleasure
Cavil, and claim her part and measure,
As if this passed with a reservation,
    Or some such words in fashion;
I here exclude the wrangler from thy treasure.   15

    O let thy sacred will
All thy delight in me fulfill!
Let me not think an action mine own way,
    But as thy love shall sway,
Resigning up the rudder to thy skill.   20

    Lord, what is man to thee,
That thou shouldst mind a rotten tree?
Yet since thou canst not choose but see my actions;
    So great are thy perfections,
Thou mayst as well my actions guide, as see.   25

    Besides, thy death and blood
Showed a strange love to all our good:
Thy sorrows were in earnest; no faint proffer,
    Or superficial offer
Of what we might not take, or be withstood.   30

Wherefore I all forgo:
To one word only I say, No:
Where in the Deed there was an intimation
Of a gift or donation,
Lord, let it now by way of purchase go.   35

He that will pass his land,
As I have mine, may set his hand
And heart unto this Deed, when he hath read;
And make the purchase spread
To both our goods, if he to it will stand.   40

How happy were my part,
If some kind man would thrust his heart
Into these lines; till in heaven's Court of Rolls
They were by winged souls
Entered for both, far above their desert!   45

The Big Picture

This poem is about obedience defined as one's unconditional surrender to God. It is cast within the framework of a conveyance made by the speaker in the writing of the poem. Both the completeness of, and the reason for, the surrender are described. Then the speaker extends an invitation for the reader to join the speaker in this conveyance. It is a poem of joyous, complete surrender to God. It is a poem of discipleship with a soft, inviting evangelical ending.

The Parts of the Picture

Stanzas 1 through 3. These stanzas define the poem as a conveyance, along with describing the elements being conveyed. The first stanza explains, and asks for acceptance of, this writing and "poor paper" as a conveyance of Lordship. Using the analogy of buyer and seller conveying property as they "please," the speaker offers up this poem as his conveyance with the hope that it "not … displease" God. Stanza 2 presents what the speaker is conveying: his heart and "all it hath." Stanza 3 removes any limitation on the conveyance despite any "cavil" or objection that may come from Pleasure. Richard Strier aptly describes the desires of the speaker: "He wants his deeding of himself to be absolute, and he solemnly discounts in advance all possible future talk of loopholes, limitations, and mental reservations."[32]

Stanzas 4 and 5. With stanza 4, there is a shift in direction. The focus is now on God's will taking over, fulfilling the speaker, and consuming the speaker's actions with His love as the speaker turns over to God's skill the rudder or steering of his life. Stanza 5 continues the theme of God's guiding of the actions of the speaker, but the method is different. While stanza 4 is a bold entreaty, stanza 5 is more of a subtle argument that goes like this: "Lord, although man is not worthy, You, with all your perfections, cannot but choose to see my actions, and so You may as well guide them, too." Stanza 4 is the direct approach with stanza 5 having a more indirect bent, but both stanzas focus on the same objective of obtaining God's acceptance of the speaker's conveyance of his heart and self and of obtaining God's guidance of the speaker's actions.

Stanzas 6 and 7. These stanzas mark another turn in the poem. Now the focus shifts to what God has done rather than on what the speaker wants done. Now the poem rests upon its reason for being: God's purchase of mankind with His "death and blood," His "strange love," His "sorrows ... in earnest." These sorrows were "no faint proffer, or superficial offer." They were offerings that were to be taken, offerings that could not be resisted or "withstood." Because of God's actions, therefore, the speaker desires to "all forgo," making clear that all of the speaker's "deed" is made possible by God's "purchase" of him rather than by any gift on the speaker's part. In short, the speaker's conveyance of himself to God is not a donation; it is, rather, made possible only by God's purchase of him.

Stanzas 8 and 9. Now Herbert does a most unusual thing for him. Although his poetry is directed to God in a manner that is likely to direct the reader to God, usually that movement by the reader is a natural by-product of the experience of reading the poem. In these two stanzas, however, Herbert extends a direct invitation to the reader to respond in a certain way. The reader may also "pass his land," just as the speaker has done in the poem, by setting "his hand and heart unto this deed, when he hath read." Such an act (a thrusting of the reader's "heart into these lines") would bring happiness to the speaker, for then the writer's and reader's "deeds" would both be entered in the registry of legal documents, far beyond what they both deserve.

The Parts of the Picture Come Together

This is a poem with a single focus and several phases. Its focus is obedient surrender to God. In the development of that focus, the poem proceeds through its phases with increasing intensity. First, there is the legal tradition. The poem begins with the idea of conveyance, the primary way of transferring ownership of "real" property in English law. It is a conveyance by which the speaker "passes" or conveys his heart and self to God. And the poet makes clear that this is done unconditionally, despite the possible objections of Pleasure. This is the offering to God.

Following the offering is the request for God to accept it. And the request is for total acceptance—may God delight the speaker with fulfillment as He takes over his thoughts, his "rudder" or steering, and his actions. But why is this done? The answer is presented—all this is done in response to the "strange love" of God revealed in His death, blood, and sorrows. Now grace transcends the law. Here the climax is reached. The speaker's life is defined by his response to this love that has "purchased" him. In that response, he conveys his all to God.

The poem could stop here. The development of its core thought is complete. Its climax has been reached. The conveyance, its content, the reasons for making it—all of these have been dealt with. But the poem goes on. In a most unusual evangelical flair for Herbert, an invitation is extended to the reader to join in the conveyance and thereby join the speaker in the heavenly hall of legal documents.

God's "strange love" for man is too large to stay within itself. It demands a response. The one who knows of this love responds with an action resembling God's action— an unconditional giving of self. But the giving does not stop there. As the poem begins with a conveyance, and as the reasons for that conveyance are revealed, the force of God's love gains such momentum that an invitation to the reader to experience that love is made as the final word.

Reflections

1. What does the poem have to say about relationship with God?
2. What spiritual direction does it provide?
3. What is inviting about the kind of obedience that the poem presents? What is difficult about it? What are its costs? Its benefits? How does one achieve it?
4. Is one's experience with, and response to, the love of God best expressed when it is merely presented (as in stanzas 1 through 7 of the poem) or should it be followed by a direct invitation to others to join in (as in stanzas 8 and 9)? Is the answer, "it depends"? If so, on what does it depend?

Scriptures for further reflection:

Isaiah 6:1-8
Luke 1:26-38
Luke 23:40-43

NOTES

CONFESSION

Sin's Round describes the process or "round" of sin as it occurs in the speaker. With vivid imagery of cabinet woodworking and moles, *Confession* gives a graphic picture of the way in which sin moves within people despite their attempts at repression. The solution, says the poem, is in the openness of confession. *Ungratefulness* confesses mankind's sin by portraying God's bountiful giving in contrast to man's ungratefulness.

SIN'S ROUND

Sorry I am, my God, sorry I am,
That my offenses course it in a ring.
My thoughts are working like a busy flame,
Until their cockatrice they hatch and bring:
And when they once have perfected their draughts,   5
My words take fire from my inflamed thoughts.

My words take fire from my inflamed thoughts,
Which spit it forth like the Sicilian Hill.
They vent the wares, and pass them with their faults,
And by their breathing ventilate the ill.   10
But words suffice not, where are lewd intentions:
My hands do joy to finish the inventions.

My hands do joy to finish the inventions:
And so my sins ascend three stories high,
As Babel grew, before there were dissensions.   15
Yet ill deeds loiter not: for they supply
New thoughts of sinning: wherefore, to my shame,
Sorry I am, my God, sorry I am.

The Big Picture

This is another of Herbert's "pattern" poems in which the pattern within the poem reflects its thought. The speaker confesses the "round" of his sins. They begin in his thoughts (first stanza), burst forth in his words (second stanza), and are then manifested through his hands. All this leads back to "new thoughts of sinning" (third stanza). This "round" is encased in the confession, "Sorry I am, my God, sorry I am."

The Parts of the Picture

The Title. A "round" indicates the movement of circular activity, and the poem is held together by the circular activity of sin.

Stanza 1. The first two lines state both the confession ("Sorry I am") and the sin being confessed ("my offenses course it [or travel] in a ring"). Lines 3-6 turn to his thoughts, to the first of the elements of the "round" of sin. These thoughts are portrayed as working like "a busy flame" that "hatch" their "cockatrice," a mythical creature depicted as a two-legged dragon with a cock's head and able to kill with its breath. This grotesque imagery vividly portrays the stark horror of the beginning round of sin. It is from these "inflamed thoughts" that his "words take fire," having "perfected their draughts [or deadly air or breath]." With all this, the first stanza has accomplished several tasks. It has established the tone of confession, stated the general nature of the problem, and described the ugliness of the beginning of sin's round in the thoughts of the speaker. It has also introduced the second phase of sin's round as thoughts begat words. To these words the second stanza turns.

Stanza 2. The pattern of the round of sin is reflected as stanzas 1 and 2 are bound together with a repetition of lines. Lines 8-10 provide the details of the destructive work of the speaker's words. These words "take fire" from the speaker's "inflamed thoughts" and "spit forth" like the volcano of a hill in Sicily (Mount Etna). These words vent (or discharge) their faulty wares (or goods) and thereby "ventilate" their ill effects. But all of this destructive intensity is not enough for the "lewd intentions" of sin. Hands now join thoughts and words to "finish" sin's "inventions."

Stanza 3. Again the stanzas are tied together with the repetition of lines as sin's round further continues. Whereas fiery imagery was used in stanzas 1 and 2 to describe the work of thoughts and words, in this stanza the imagery of height is used to reflect the work of hands. Hands build, and hence the work of hands ascends as did another work of sin, the Tower of Babel (Genesis 11). Although sin's round is now complete (thoughts linked to words and words to deeds), it does not stop. Just as thoughts begat fiery words and those fiery words begat ascending deeds, these deeds now beget "new thoughts of sinning," and the round begins again as the speaker closes with the same confessional lament that began the poem.

The Parts of the Picture Come Together

We go no farther than the title to discover how the parts of this poem come together. The movement is simply in a round. Just as simply, sin drives the round. It is the same round of sin described in the confession in the Book of Common Prayer: "We have erred in thought, word, and deed.…" The round is tightly enclosed, encased in the lament that begins and ends the poem. The stanzas are tied together by the repetition of lines. In a circular movement, the imagery intensifies in stanza 1 (with "inflamed thoughts"), then bursts forth in stanza 2 (as the "words take fire" from these thoughts), then ascends like Babel in stanza 3 (with the work of the hands), and finally begins the round again in line 17 (with a return to "new thoughts").

The final product is a picture of sin at work. And all of this is taking place within and through a person who takes responsibility for the sin as he begins and ends with his sorrow. Maybe it is in this beginning and ending expression of sorrow that something other than sin is at work in the poem. Perhaps (though certainly the poem does not *di-*

rectly comment on this) this is the hope (if there is any) in the poem. Despite the horrifying fiery power of sin that strikes out and ascends as it moves round, perhaps confession is the beginning of the end of the cycle. Perhaps the poem attests, through its confessional mode, that the only way out of the vicious cycle of sin is assuming responsibility for it. After all, the poem is a prayer, and for Herbert, there is always hope in prayer.

Reflections

1. What does the poem have to say about relationship with God?
2. What spiritual direction does it provide?
3. How do you react to the "round of sin" portrayed in the poem? How would you describe the pattern (or patterns) that sin takes in your life?
4. What do you find to be the best way(s) of breaking the round of sin?

Scriptures for further reflection:

Genesis 3
Proverbs 5:22
Isaiah 43:25
Micah 7:19
John 8:34-36
Romans 3:23
Romans 6:8-14 and 23
Romans 7:14-25
Hebrews 12:1

CONFESSION

O what a cunning guest
Is this same grief! within my heart I made
 Closets; and in them many a chest;
 And, like a master in my trade,
In those chests, boxes; in each box, a till: 5
Yet grief knows all, and enters when he will.

 No screw, no piercer can
Into a piece of timber work and wind,
 As God's afflictions into man,
 When he a torture hath designed.   10
They are too subtle for the subtlest hearts;
And fall, like rheums, upon the tenderest parts.

 We are the earth; and they,
Like moles within us, heave, and cast about:
 And till they foot and clutch their prey,   15
 They never cool, much less give out.
No smith can make such locks but they have keys:
Closets are hall to them; and hearts, highways.

 Only an open breast
Doth shut them out, so that they cannot enter;   20
 Or, if they enter, cannot rest,
 But quickly seek some new adventure.
Smooth open hearts no fastening have; but fiction
Doth give a hold and handle to affliction.

 Wherefore my faults and sins,   25
Lord, I acknowledge; take thy plagues away:
 For since confession pardon wins
 I challenge here the brightest day,
The clearest diamond: let them do their best,
They shall be thick and cloudy to my breast.   30

The Big Picture

Psalm 32:3-5 provides a good statement of the theme of this poem: "When I kept silence…thy hand was heavy upon me… I acknowledged my sin unto thee…and thou forgavest… my sin." The poem rests upon a paradox: opening, not closing, protects. In short, confession succeeds where repression fails. Affliction (related to the repression of sin) assaults the heart. All of man's contrived ways to close the heart, and thereby protect it, fail to do so. Ironically, it is the open heart, the confessing heart, that protects. Therefore, in closing the poem, the speaker opens his heart with his confession—and rejoices in the release.

The Parts of the Picture

"Grief". Although this term is often associated with the feelings experienced as a result of a significant loss, in this poem it has the broader meaning of the discomfort, frustration, and unrest that arises without regard to a loss. Within this poem, the term is used to indicate something more akin to guilt. It is used synonymously with "God's afflictions" (line 9), "affliction" (line 24), and the Lord's "plagues" (line 26) that result from an attempt by the speaker to hide or repress his sin. Indeed, the first three stanzas describe the "grief" of the failed effort to hide sin, and the final two describe the release that comes from this "grief" as a result of confession.

Stanza 1. The problem is presented. "Grief" is described as "a cunning guest" that "knows all" and "enters when he will," despite the elaborate system of closets, chests, boxes, and tills (compartments used to store valuables) that the speaker has built for protection within his heart.

Stanzas 2-3. Several images portray the workings of grief or "God's afflictions." First, these afflictions are more powerful than tools made for piercing wood. But not only do they pierce, they are also "subtle," like a mucous discharge falling on the most tender parts of the heart. In addition to boring in like a screw or seeping in like mucous, these afflictions "heave and cast about" in us like moles in the earth. Like moles they are never relenting until they "foot" (or seize) "their prey." And finally these afflictions are represented as having keys, opening locks so that closets (referred to in line 3) are opened into hallways and hearts become unimpeded highways for these invaders.

Stanza 4. The poem turns. There is a solution. It is both surprising and striking: "an open breast/ Doth shut them out [emphasis added]." It is the breast or heart that has opened itself in confession that can keep out these afflictions or, if they enter, makes them restless so that they seek other adventures. The couplet in lines 23-24 provides a summary contrast of "Smooth open hearts" (to which nothing fastens since they have confessed and thereby released their sins) and hearts full of fiction or untruths (perhaps denials of sin) to which afflictions can hold.

Stanza 5. The speaker puts his solution into action and confesses. By confessing he enables his heart to be so bright and clear that even the brightest day and the clearest diamond will seem "thick and cloudy" when compared to it.

The Parts of the Picture Come Together

There are three forces that drive this poem: the extensive but unsuccessful effort of the speaker to protect his heart; the unrelenting invasive force of grief; and the victorious release issuing from confession.

Initially the speaker establishes an elaborate defense system described in terms of closets, chests, boxes, and compartments to fortify his heart against the invasive force of "God's afflictions." As Richard Strier points out, "The imagery of craftsmanship here expresses the intensity... of the 'natural' human desire to withdraw or withhold from God, to establish and maintain a place in the self apart from Him.... Ingenuity, subtlety seeks to lock the heart...from God."[33] But to no avail, as the first stanza concludes: "Yet grief...enters when he will."

The poem gains intensity as the speaker turns away from his own efforts and focuses on the power of grief caused by unconfessed sin's invasive workings. Four comparisons are used to portray these workings.

Afflictions "pierce" in a manner greater than screws into wood.

Afflictions "seep" like mucous on the most tender parts of a heart.

Afflictions "heave and cast about" like moles in the earth, relentlessly seizing their prey.

Afflictions, like keys, "unlock" the locks secured by a locksmith. Piercing, seeping, heaving, unlocking—quite the picture of repressed sin at work.

Now the focus of the poem turns again. There is a resolution to this problem—but only one: "only an open breast/Doth shut them out." Here is the paradox on which the poem rests. It is the openness of confession that dissolves the forces of repressed sin, that drives the afflictions to unrest, that smooths the heart of all things to which this kind of grief may attach. Hence, it is to confession that the speaker turns. He participates in the resolution. He now embodies the energy of the poem. Armed with the power provided by pardon, he now is the challenger (rather that being overwhelmed as he was in stanzas 1-3). And he challenges the brightest day and the clearest diamond—even at their best they are thick and cloudy compared to his cleansed breast.

What a turnaround! The poem starts with the despair of grief, an affliction that penetrates, seeps, causes upheaval, and unlocks places thought secure. Then the reversal comes with a release, the release of confession that opens and cleanses the heart and transforms the speaker from the one challenged to the one challenging. From the despair and paralysis of being afflicted, to the cleansing of confession that energizes and challenges, to the brightness and clarity of the victory of pardon—the speaker has experienced the transformation of confession.

Reflections

1. What does this poem have to say about relationship with God?
2. What spiritual direction does it provide?
3. In what way(s) are your experiences similar to and/or different from those of the speaker in this poem? How would you describe your attempts to repress or deny your sins? How would you describe the effects of those efforts? How would you describe the effects of confession?
4. Is confession difficult for you? Or, stated another way, is denial of sin easy for you? If so, why? Must we be brought to confession by the power of "God's afflictions" as described in this poem, or is there another way? Or does it all depend on the nature of the sin we are dealing with?

Scriptures for further reflection:

Psalms 32:1-5
Psalms 51
Psalms 130
John 1:8-10

Ungratefulness

Lord, with what bounty and rare clemency
      Hast thou redeemed us from the grave!
          If thou hadst let us run,
      Gladly had man adored the sun,
          And thought his god most brave;   5
Where now we shall be better gods than he.

Thou hast but two rare cabinets full of treasure,
      The Trinity, and Incarnation:
          Thou hast unlocked them both,
      And made them jewels to betroth   10
          The work of thy creation
Unto thy self in everlasting pleasure.

The statelier cabinet is the Trinity,
      Whose sparkling light access denies:
          Therefore thou dost not show   15
      This fully to us, till death blow
          The dust into our eyes:
For by that powder thou will make us see.

But all thy sweets are packed up in the other;
      Thy mercies thither flock and flowers: 20
          That as the first affrights,
      This may allure us with delights;
          Because this box we know;
For we have all of us just such another.

But man is close, reserved, and dark to thee: 25
      When thou demandest but a heart,
          He cavils instantly.
      In his poor cabinet of bone
          Sins have their box apart,
Defrauding thee, who gavest two for one.   30

The Big Picture

This poem comments on the actions of God and man. A large portion of the poem portrays God as a bountiful and merciful giver who has given two great gifts: the Trinity and the Incarnation. In contrast, there is man's ungrateful response to God's gracious offering.

The Parts of the Picture

Stanza 1. The first note is one of praise to the Lord for the "bounty" and "rare clemency" (God's mercy) by which He has redeemed his creatures. Lines 3-6 state the results of God's action. If God had not acted in this way, man would have fallen into idolatry (sun worship); but because God has acted in this way, man "shall be better gods" than the sun (see Matthew 13:43 where Jesus concludes his explanation of a parable by stating that after the judgment the righteous "shine forth as the sun in the kingdom of their Father"; see also Daniel 12:3).

Stanza 2 introduces the details of God's gracious action. He has "unlocked" His "two rare cabinets full of treasure," the Trinity and the Incarnation. Through these two "jewels," God has wedded mankind ("the work of thy creation") to Himself "in everlasting pleasure." The stage is now set for a more detailed description of these "two rare cabinets" in the next two stanzas.

Stanza 3 deals with the Trinity, "the statelier cabinet," access to which is denied by its "sparkling light." This is the transcendent, the mysterious dimension of God. This aspect of God will not be revealed completely to us until "death blow / The dust into our eyes," an allusion to the common treatment of blowing powder into the bad eyes of a horse or dog to clear the film.

Stanza 4. Although we are denied access to the first of God's cabinets, and even though that first cabinet "affrights" us, the second cabinet, the Incarnation, "allures us with delights." In this cabinet are God's "sweets" or pleasures and appealing delights. We are familiar with "this box," for all of us have a body.

Stanza 5. Mankind's response to these gifts is to be "close, reserv'd, and dark" to God. These characteristics of man are the opposite of God's "bounty and rare clemency" (line 1), of God's unlocking His two "rare cabinets" (line 9), and of God's mercies flowing (line 20). While God desires man's heart, man "cavils instantly." This mocking of God with petty objections is the essence of "ungratefulness." Furthermore, this action comes to man "instantly." It is his natural reaction. In contrast to God's "two rare cabinets full of treasure" (line 7), man's "poor cabinet of bone" (line 28) contains sins' "box apart." It is these sins, their box in contrast to God's "two rare cabinets," that "defraud" God who has given two great gifts and asks only for man's heart in return.

The Parts of the Picture Come Together

The unfolding of this poem in the first four stanzas proceeds in well-ordered, joyous praise of God. There is general praise for God's redeeming goodness and mercy toward man. This is followed by a description of the particulars by which God has wedded Himself to His creation. There is the Trinity, shrouded in mystery, only partially revealed to us on this earth. And there is the Incarnation when the Word became flesh and dwelt among us. This flesh we understand as it "allures us with delights." This part of the poem is spoken to God, spoken in praise of God, spoken full of joyous admiration of God's redeeming bounty.

Then the poem takes a dramatic, sudden, surprising, dark turn. All that God expects in return for His gracious movement toward man is man's heart. But all that God receives is man's ungratefulness. Such a difference. It is a change rooted in sin's defrauding God. Ungratefulness works that way.

But why does the poem work this way? Why is the poem so seemingly unbalanced with its content? That is, why is so much space given to God's nature and so little to man's? If the poem is about "ungratefulness," why is not most of the poem devoted to that subject rather than to God's goodness and grace? There is, of course, no way of knowing the answers to these questions, but we can speculate about them and that might be helpful in coming to a better understanding and appreciation of the way in which the poem comes together.

Perhaps the best way of talking about man's ungratefulness is, first, to establish the context out of which it emerges. Or put another way, for the reader to understand man's failure to be grateful, he must first understand that for which man should be grateful. For Herbert, man is always living in response to what God has done and is doing. It is always within the context of God's actions that man's actions are to be evaluated. Hence, it is natural for Herbert to begin with God.

And maybe, also, it is a matter of emphasis. That is to say, perhaps the best way to emphasize the magnitude of man's ungratefulness is to give it a small showing in contrast to the spacious breadth and depth of God's grace. In fact, that is the point of the poem. What God has done is of the grandest magnitude; in contrast, what man has done is small, or "close, reserv'd, and dark," as the poem says. God has "two rare cabinets full of treasure"; man has only "his poor cabinet of bone" in which "sins have their box apart." Since this great contrast is at the heart of the poem, perhaps the best way of emphasizing it is by devoting most of the poem to God's actions.

And, perhaps most importantly, Herbert wanted the reader to learn more about God than about man. Or put another way, perhaps he wanted the reader to be drawn to God rather than merely to be repelled by man's actions. To be sure, the poem is meant to be convicting about the matter of man's ungratefulness, but Herbert's desire is not merely to ridicule and certainly not to be cynical or sarcastic. Instead, as the poem convicts man for his ungratefulness, it also gives the reader something of great attraction, something to "allure us with delights." Naturally, therefore, the poet would devote most of the poem to that alluring subject matter.

Reflections

1. What does the poem have to say about relationship with God?
2. What spiritual direction does it provide?
3. What is the purpose of the poem? To praise? To lament? To instruct? To convict? Something else? All of these?
4. Why is the poem directed to God? Why not to man? Or is it directed to man? Or to both man and God?
5. How do you discover your ungratefulness? How do you deal with it?
6. Herbert took a certain approach to ungratefulness in this poem. If you were writing about it, what approach would you take?

Scriptures for further reflection:

Deuteronomy 31:20
Isaiah 5:1-4
Hosea 11:1-4
Matthew 23:37-39
Luke 16:19-31
Luke 17:11-19

GRACE

*T*hese four poems deal with the heart of Herbert's spirituality: God's grace. Using allegory, the speaker in *Redemption* tells a story embodying grace. *Dialogue* uses the conversation between the speaker and Jesus to portray the power of grace to overcome the speaker's sense of unworthiness. *Judgment* and *Love (III)* utilize the context of entering into heaven to give Herbert's final word on grace in his collection of poetry in *The Temple*.

REDEMPTION

Having been tenant long to a rich Lord,
  Not thriving, I resolved to be bold,
  And make a suit unto him, to afford
A new small-rented lease, and cancel the old.
In heaven at his manor I him sought: 5
  They told me there, that he was lately gone
  About some land, which he had dearly bought
Long since on earth, to take possession.
I straight returned, and knowing his great birth,
  Sought him accordingly in great resorts;   10
  In cities, theaters, gardens, parks, and courts:
At length I heard a ragged noise and mirth
  Of thieves and murderers: there I him espied,
  Who straight, Your suit is granted, said, and died.

The Big Picture

In allegorical fashion, this poem tells a story of a quest. There is only one character until the last two lines when the story takes an abrupt turn with the introduction of the second character who does all his work in one line. Despite being limited to one line. He becomes the main character. It is a story about the old and the new, works and grace, and man's ways with God. And it is a story about one of God's ways with man: redemption.

The Parts of the Picture

The Divisions. Lines 1-4 describe the context and content of the narrator's resolve to seek out the "new." The next four lines (5-8) set this resolution into action by describing the seeking and the first discovery of the narrator in heaven. Lines 9-12 continue the seeking, this time on earth. In line 12, there is an abrupt shift beginning with "ragged." The closing couplet concludes the quest as the narrator finds the "rich Lord" who grants the narrator's desire—but in a radically different way than anticipated.

The Parts of the Picture Come Together

The movement of the poem is from the "old" (lines 1-2) to the narrator's resolve to bring forth the "new" (lines 3-4). The quest (lines 5-12) is toward the "new," using the works and wisdom of the narrator. As the quest by the narrator culminates in the "new" (lines 13-14), it is a newness wrought not by the narrator but by the "rich Lord."

Since this is a poem about the triumph of grace over works, it is no surprise that irony is significant throughout. In a most important sense, the ironies of the poem function around the irony of grace itself. For example: (1) the narrator's whole resolve rests on his determined self-sufficiency; but his quest comes to fruition only through the grace of the rich Lord; (2) the "richness" of the Lord is defined by what He gives away; (3) the narrator seeks the rich Lord in the "right" places (as defined by society) but finds him in the midst of death and murderers and thieves; (4) the narrator's request is granted before it is presented; and (5) the land is "dearly bought" in a manner completely unexpected by the narrator.

The climax of the story comes in the final irony of the sudden, unexpected breakdown of the narrator's worldview. In lines 1-12a, the narrator asserts his control through reasoning and determined, self-sufficient action. Beginning, however, with "ragged" in line 12, his world is lost—and redeemed by!—the unimaginable action of the Lord. The human effort to control is subsumed in the mystery of God's grace.

Reflections

1. What does the poem have to say about relationship with God?
2. What spiritual direction does the poem provide?
3. What reminders and/or new discoveries does the poem provide concerning the following:
   a. The extent to which we live out of (and thereby have our identities shaped by) our works as opposed to living out of God's grace?
   b. The sudden and mysterious nature of God's ways and the manner in which they radically alter, and thereby ironically fulfill, our best-laid plans?
   c. Our willingness or unwillingness to allow our self-centered worlds to be redeemed as we "him espy" (line 13)?
4. How do you react to this comment about the poem:
   "Redemption' dramatizes not only the strangeness of the means of grace but also the strange givenness of grace."
5. Do you find any relationship between this poem and the following advice given to a class of seminary students:
   "As Christians, we are indeed called to good works and questing after God, but primarily and ultimately we are called to live out of God's grace. My prayer for you is that you will learn to live out of God's grace."

Scriptures for further reflection:

Luke 24:13-32	II Corinthians 3:6
Hebrews 8:6-13	Colossians 2:13-14

DIALOGUE

Sweetest Saviour, if my soul
      Were but worth the having,
Quickly should I then control
      And thought of waving.
But when all my care and pains   5
Cannot give the name of gains
To thy wretch so full of stains,
What delight or hope remains?

What, Child, is the balance thine,
      Thine the poise and measure?   10
If I say, Thou shalt be mine;
      Finger not my treasure.
What the gains in having thee
Do amount to, only he,
Who for man was sold, can see;   15
That transferred the accounts to me.

But as I can see no merit,
      Leading to this favor:
So the way to fit me for it
      Is beyond my savour.   20
As the reason then is thine;
So the way is none of mine:
I disclaim the whole design:
Sin disclaims and I resign.

That is all, if that I could   25
      Get without repining;
And my clay, my creature, would
      Follow my resigning:
That as I did freely part
With my glory and desert,   30
Left all joys to feel all smart – –
      Ah! No more: thou breakest my heart.

The Big Picture

This poem presents two opposing answers to the question of what makes one worthy. In short, it contrasts works and grace, man's view of worth as opposed to God's. The presentation is in the form of a debate with the speaker stating his position and then a rebuttal by Jesus. This is repeated with the debate finally being resolved when grace happens and the speaker is overcome by the sacrifice of Christ.

The Parts of the Picture

Stanza 1. The speaker presents his case. In addressing the Savior in lines 1-4, he makes clear that if his "soul" were "worth having," he would "control" or eliminate any thought of "waving" or declining Jesus' offer, presumably the offer of "having" or saving the speaker's soul. Clearly for the speaker the issue is worthiness—and the speaker condemns his worth. In reality (lines 5-8), the speaker contends, his situation is without delight or hope. In effect, all the efforts of the speaker (his "care and pains") have failed to produce any "gains," and he remains a wretch "full of stains." His plight is tightly bound in the rhyming of "pains," "gains," "stains," and "remains" at the end of lines 5-8.

Stanza 2. The Savior replies and shifts the focus. He challenges the assumptions of the speaker. Are the matters of "balance," "poise," and "measure" the speaker's ("child")? Certainly not. The speaker is the Savior's treasure, and if He says the speaker shall be his, the speaker is to release His "finger" or grip on himself. The real issue is ownership and not worthiness. Hence, the Savior clarifies the ownership issue and claims His own. The Savior determines the "gains" of having the speaker. Only the One "who for man was sold" (as in Judas's betrayal and or as in Jesus' becoming a "ransom for many") has the right to determine the worth of man. The Savior's action has transferred man's "accounts" to Him.

Stanza 3. But the speaker is unconvinced. He clings to his unworthiness. He can see no "merit" on his part "Leading to" or opening the way to the Savior's "favor" bestowed on him. He, therefore, declares it beyond his ability to understand ("savor") how there could be any way (as in "manner" or possibly an allusion, unknown to the speaker, to Jesus as the Way) to "fit" (or make him worthy) of this "favor." Then comes the speaker's disclaimer (lines 21-24). Because the reason and the way (again an allusion to Jesus as the Way?) for all of this is the Savior's and not the speaker's, and because Sin "disclaims" or refuses the Savior's reasoning, the speaker "resigns" or removes himself from the debate. Unless the way and the reason are his, he will exit. Control he must.

Stanza 4. But the Savior will have his rebuttal. The speaker has announced his resignation (line 24). Ironically, the poem turns on this. "Resignation" is exactly where the Savior wants the debate to be. This is the ultimate issue, not worthiness. Resignation is precisely what Jesus wants from the speaker if He can get it without the speaker's regret or reservation (lines 25-26). Indeed, He wants the speaker ("my clay, my creature") to follow His model of resigning when He freely parted from his "glory and desert" (or what he deserved) and left His joys to "feel all smart" or feel all the pain of the Cross. The poem jolts to a conclusion. The Savior has made His point. The speaker now truly resigns, this time in the manner the Savior desires. He asks for mercy: "Ah! No more." His heart is broken, his defiance gone. He is now the Lord's. Grace has triumphed over the ways of worthiness.

The Parts of the Picture Come Together

The dynamics of this debate intensify as the poem moves to and through three surrenders. The first movement begins with "Sweetest Savior," revealing the warm, intimate lure of Jesus. But rather than submitting to this attractive Savior, the speaker wants to control the situation. The desire to "let go" is there. But there is a problem—worthiness. Hence, the expression of sweetness is rapidly displaced by the despair of the speaker's wretchedness, his pains and stains, his lack of "gains." This shift in perspective is the core of the speaker's stance. With his focus on Jesus, there is sweetness; but when he chooses to shift that focus to himself, delight is gone. With the conclusion of the first movement of his argument, the speaker has turned from the sweetness of Jesus to the dismay of his own world of failure. This is the first surrender, a surrender by the speaker to the despair of his unworthiness.

The Savior replies. His rebuttal turns another way. Intimately addressing his "child," the Savior strikes hard. "You've got it all wrong," He admonishes. In short, He tries to change the speaker's focus. The issue is not what the speaker has done. The issue is what the Savior has done. The speaker belongs to the Savior, and He will determine the issue of gains and worthiness. He has taken over the accounts of man.

But the speaker hangs tough. Like a puppy holding fiercely to a sock in a tug of war with his master for possession, the speaker intensifies his opposition to the Savior. He returns to the issue of his own worthiness. He understands that. That is his way. Since the Savior has His own reasons and way, the speaker adamantly disclaims the whole debate. This is the second surrender, but again in the wrong manner and to the wrong thing. He resigns. He will walk away from all of this.

But not so. The Savior speaks again, and this time he will stay with the issue stated by the speaker. "Yes," let's talk about resignation," the Savior says. But as the Savior stays with the issue of resignation, He shifts to His own kind of resignation. If the speaker wants to resign, he needs to consider how the Savior resigned, leaving all his glory for the "smart" or pain of the Incarnation. That is true resignation.

Here, abruptly, the argument stops. Here real surrender takes place in the speaker's heart as he realizes the Savior's surrender, a surrender of the glory of heaven in order to become flesh and die for mankind. The movement of the poem is complete. Argument ceases as the pain and peace of a broken heart emerges. Merit has given way to grace. Reason has been subdued by agape love. The Savior has claimed His treasure on His own terms. The speaker surrenders with a broken and contrite heart, the sure way to God.

Reflections

1. What does the poem have to say about relationship with God?
2. What spiritual direction does it provide?
3. How real for you is the debate in this poem? In effect, how do you react to the debate about grace and merit, about our unworthiness and God's acceptance of us nonetheless, about our insistence on looking at things our way in determining our worth instead of surrendering to God's way?
4. Why does the speaker make the arguments he does in stanzas 1 and 3? What is the nature of the harm done to our relationship with God by these kinds of arguments? Do you ever find yourself thinking in a manner similar to the speaker's?

Scriptures for further reflection:

Exodus 3:9-4:20
Isaiah 6:1-8
Philippians 2:5-8

JUDGMENT

Almighty Judge, how shall poor wretches brook
                    Thy dreadful look,
Able a heart of iron to appall,
                    When thou shalt call
          For every man's peculiar book?   5

What others mean to do, I know not well;
                    Yet I hear tell,
That some will turn thee to some leaves therein
                    So void of sin,
          That they in merit shall excel.   10

But I resolve, when thou shalt call for mine,
                    That to decline,
And thrust a Testament into thy hand;
                    Let that be scanned.
          There thou shalt find my faults are thine.   15

The Big Picture

What a delightful poem on a most serious subject! The scene is set. The speaker stands before the "Almighty Judge." What will he do? Although some in that situation may argue their case based on their accomplishments, the speaker takes another approach.

The Parts of the Picture

Stanza 1. The poem is directed to the "Almighty Judge." The issue concerns how "poor wretches" will be able to "brook" or tolerate the Judge's dreadful look that is able to appall or horrify a heart of iron on Judgment Day when the Judge shall call for every person's "peculiar book" or record of his life.

Stanza 2. The speaker reports that he has heard that some will point to "leaves" or pages in the person's book that will testify to the merit of the individual.

Stanza 3. The speaker makes clear his resolution to the problem of standing before the Judge. Instead of relying on any merits in his own "book," the speaker will present another book, a Testament (see Hebrews 9: 14-15), that provides the answer to the problem of standing before the Judge. In that New Testament, the Judge will find that He has taken on the "faults" of the speaker.

The Parts of the Picture Come Together

The movement of the poem is typical of Herbert. First, a problem is posed and then options are explored in search of a resolution. All of this is compressed into 15 lines. The conclusion is pure Reformation justification theology of salvation by grace through faith (Romans 3:20-23, Galatians 2:15-21, Ephesians 2:8-9).

The problem presented concerns facing the Almighty Judge when He calls for everyone's book of life. A confluence of striking images poses the problem. First, there is the Almighty Judge with a "dreadful look," holding every man accountable for his "peculiar book." Then there are "poor wretches" caught in this "dreadful look." In light of all this, what is a person to do?

The speaker speaks first of what he has heard some will do. It is the argument of good works. Those who choose this way will guide the Judge's attention to the pages of their book that are "void of sin." On the merit of their accomplishments, these people hope to resolve the problem of judgment.

But not so for the speaker. Since there is no justification in his book, he declines to present it. What he will present, instead, is "a Testament," one which resolves the problem with a paradox: the faults of the one judged have been claimed by the Judge (see Hebrews 9:15). This is the paradox of the Christian faith, the grace of the loving God revealed in Jesus Christ who has taken unto Himself the faults of His creatures. Here is the resolution of the Judgment.

Reflections

1. What does the poem have to say about relationship with God?
2. What spiritual direction does it provide?
3. How prevalent is the idea of justifying our personhood by our good works? Stated another way, what approximate percentage of the people you know base their self worth on their works or accomplishments? The question has both a psychological dimension (concerning the basis of our self-esteem) and a spiritual dimension (concerning the basis of how we see ourselves standing before God). Answer the question by addressing both these dimensions.
4. Do you find yourself attracted to or involved in this kind of self-justification by works? If so, why?
5. What do you think the seminary professor meant when he advised his students to "live and minister out of God's grace and not on the basis of your accomplishments"?

Scriptures for further reflection:

Romans 3:20-23

Ephesians 2:8-9

Galatians 2:15-21

Revelation 20:12

LOVE (III)

Love bade me welcome: yet my soul drew back,
    Guilty of dust and sin.
But quick-eyed Love, observing me grow slack
    From my first entrance in,
Drew nearer to me, sweetly questioning,   5
    If I lacked any thing.

A guest, I answered, worthy to be here:
    Love said, You shall be he.
I the unkind, ungrateful? Ah my dear,
    I cannot look on thee.   10
Love took my hand, and smiling did reply,
    Who made the eyes but I?

Truth Lord, but I have marred them: let my shame
    Go where it doth deserve.
And know you not, says Love, who bore the blame?   15
    My dear, then I will serve.
You must sit down, says Love, and taste my meat:
    So I did sit and eat.

The Big Picture

This poem encompasses several elements. It is, as Joseph Summers states succinctly, "a description of the soul's reception into heaven."[38] And as Louis Martz points out, it is "the reception of the redeemed at 'the marriage supper of the Lamb' (Rev. 19:9) as well as the administration of the Communion service."[39] The poem works itself out in the context of a meal with strong Eucharistic overtones. A grand picture of grace unfolds as the guest and host move through their dialogue.

The Parts of the Picture

Stanza 1. Here is the tension at the heart of the poem: Love welcomes the speaker, but the speaker draws back because of his sense of guilt. Love's response is to draw nearer, inquiring "sweetly" of the speaker's needs.

Stanza 2. The speaker emerges more. He reveals his deficiency. What is lacking is worthiness. But Love assures him that he shall be a worthy guest. The speaker is not persuaded. He cannot even "look on" Love. But Love's response is to close whatever gap there is between them. Love takes the speaker's hand with a smiling reply and picks up on the imagery of sight introduced by the speaker by pointing out that it is He who is in charge of looking since He has made the speaker's eyes.

Stanza 3. As the poem moves toward resolution, the speaker has the first word, and, again, it is a word of separation. But Love has the last word, and this is a word of reconciliation. The rhetorical question makes clear that Love has taken care of the issue of blame. With a reference to Love as "My dear" (as in line 9), the speaker insists on serving the meal. But Love makes clear that the speaker is to sit and taste. And so the speaker does "sit and eat."

The Parts of the Picture Come Together

The forces arrayed against each other in this poem are powerful indeed. On the one side are Love and Grace welcoming the speaker, offering to meet his needs, persisting with concern, and desiring to embrace their guest. On the other side is guilt with its accompanying sense of unworthiness and desire to withdraw.

The tension is resolved through two movements working within the poem. The tightness of the exchanges in the dialogue between Love and the speaker drives the first movement. This movement goes back and forth between Love and the speaker with the intensity building as it moves to its resolution in the final lines. The second movement, however, pushes consistently straight ahead. This movement is embodied in Love's persistent argument for the speaker to join the feast. The speaker's resistance based on his unworthiness finally succumbs to the grace embodied in Love's insistence.

The poem begins with separation between Love and the speaker. Often it is the pride or the denial of sins committed that causes the separation. But here the foe is the speaker's sense of unworthiness. The separation is stated quickly, directly. In response to Love's welcome, the speaker recoils, driven by his guilt rooted in His mortality and sin. But just as quickly and directly, Love moves to bridge the divide, driven by Love's desire to meet the speaker's need. The movement is compact: Love welcomes; the speaker rejects; Love draws nearer. The issue is worthiness.

The next movement is again compressed. The speaker restates his position. Love's retort is rapid, as is yet another statement of unworthiness by the speaker: "I cannot look on thee." But Love is undaunted and moves forward without pause, taking the speaker's hand and smilingly pointing out that it is Love who controls the speaker's power to see since Love made his eyes. In the tightness and intensity of the exchanges, Love never fails. But against the unceasing advance of Love, the speaker, like a puppy clinging to a sock in a tug-of-war with his master, tenaciously holds onto his unworthiness as he demands to receive what his shame deserves.

The last word, however, belongs to Love. The issue of blame is removed. Love has borne it already. One last time the speaker insists on his way. He will submit and join the meal, but he will serve the meal. Love's His H directive to the speaker, however, is blunt and forceful: sit and taste. (See Luke 12:37) Finally the speaker submits unconditionally. The speaker finally receives. The separation is removed. The power of guilt is vacated. Love's persistence prevails. It's that way with Grace. Now the speaker may "sit and eat"—and he does.

Reflections

1. What does the poem have to say about relationship with God?
2. What spiritual direction does it provide?
3. The poem deals with one of those elements that separate us from God—a sense of unworthiness. Has a sense of unworthiness played itself out in your relationship with God and/or with other persons? How would you describe it? How do you deal with it?
4. The issue of our unworthiness can be viewed as a self-help issue. That is, our secular culture encourages us to resolve the issue within our self. But the poem takes a different approach in that the strongest force within the poem is the Love of God that beckons the speaker to partake of the gift of the meal without regard to his sense of unworthiness. How do you respond to these differing approaches? Are they mutually exclusive or is there the possibility of a merger? If so, how?

Scriptures for further reflection:

Isaiah 25:6-9
Matthew 22:1-10
Luke 13:29
Luke 15:1-2
John 13:1-9
Revelation 19:6-9

SEPARATION

These poems deal with the feelings of being separated from God. This experience, along with the experience of grace and the proclaiming of praise, is part of the journey with God, the working out of our salvation. So it was with Herbert. *The Search* portrays an intimate, passionate (almost desperate) search for the God who has fled. *Denial* is a petition for God to hear the speaker's plea. *Church Lock and Key* is cast in a different tone, with more confidence expressed in the power of Christ's blood to unlock the damage done by the speaker's sin.

THE SEARCH

Whither, O, whither art thou fled,
             My Lord, my Love?
My searches are my daily bread;
             Yet never prove.

My knees pierce the earth, mine eyes the sky;   5
             And yet the sphere
And center both to me deny
             That thou art there.

Yet can I mark how herbs below
             Grow green and gay,   10
As if to meet thee they did know,
             While I decay.

Yet can I mark how stars above
             Simper and shine,
As having keys unto thy love,   15
             While poor I pine.

I sent a sigh to seek thee out,
             Deep drawn in pain,
Winged like an arrow: but my scout
             Returns in vain.   20

I tuned another (having store)
             Into a groan;
Because the search was dumb before:
             But all was one.

Lord, dost thou some new fabric mold,   25
             Which favour wins,
And keeps thee present, leaving the old
             Unto their sins?

Where is my God? What hidden place
                    Conceals thee still?
What covert dare eclipse thy face?
                    Is it thy will?   30

O let not that of any thing;
                    Let rather brass,
Or steel, or mountains be thy ring,
                    And I will pass.   35

Thy will such an entrenching is,
                    As passeth thought:
To it all strength, all subtleties
                    Are things of nought.   40

Thy will such a strange distance is,
                    As that to it
East and West touch, the poles do kiss,
                    And parallels meet.

Since then my grief must be as large,   45
                    As is thy space,
Thy distance from me; see my charge,
                    Lord, see my case.

O take these bars, these lengths away;
                    Turn, and restore me: 50
Be not Almighty, let me say,
                    Against, but for me.

When thou dost turn, and wilt be near;
                    What edge so keen,
What point so piercing can appear   55
                    To come between?

For as thy absence doth excel
                    All distance known:
So doth thy nearness bear the bell,
                    Making two one.   60

The Big Picture

"Here is a passionate search after God."[40] These words of 18th century critic George Ryley aptly describe this poem. Contained in this poem/prayer are the desires, the questions, the pleadings, the frustrations, the sadness, the seeking, and the passion of one searching fruitlessly for God. It concludes with a statement of the value of God's presence.

The Parts of the Picture

Stanzas 1 and 2. With a question, the first two lines make apparent God's absence. The address in line 2, "My Lord, My Love," sets the tone of the poem. Indeed this is a passionate search but also a tender one. Lines 3-6 describe his "searches." They are his "daily bread," yet the bread never rises (or "prove"). He pierces earth and sky, yet God is not found.

Stanzas 3-4. The speaker contrasts his condition with that of the natural world. He decays while the herbs prosper. He pines while the stars act as if they have the keys to God's love.

Stanzas 5-6. The speaker's efforts with sighs and groans are recorded. In Sion Herbert stated that nothing is so dear to God as "one good groan." Not so here. The speaker's sigh returned "in vain" while another was sent as a groan but there was silence again.

Stanzas 7-8. The speaker turns from making statements about his condition to asking questions (for the first time since lines 2 and 3). Has God turned away his "old" creatures in their sins and started to mold "some new fabric"? What "hidden place/Conceals" God? What covering ("covert") dares to hide God's face? And then the most important question of all—is it God's will that does this?

Stanzas 9-11. God's will is the focus here. That the cause of God's silence is God's will is the most dreaded possibility "of anything." He had rather God be "ringed" or concealed by brass, or steel, or mountains because the speaker would pass through those. But God's will is another matter. It is such an "entrenching" (an entrenching firmly established) that "all strength, all subtleties" come to naught went arrayed against it. In short, the changing of God's will is beyond the strength or wit of the speaker. Another aspect of God's will (stanza 11) is that its distance is "strange" or as unimaginable as east and west touching, or the north and south "kissing," or parallel lines meeting.

Stanzas 12-15. As the poem concludes, the speaker returns to petitioning, recognizing that it is only God who can remove the barriers. The plea to God is direct: turn, restore me, and be for, and not against, me. The final two stanzas conclude the speaker's plea by declaring the benefits of the return of God's presence. This declaration comes subtly in stanza 14 through a rhetorical question. What point or edge could pry apart

God and the speaker if He returns? Stanza 15 ends the plea with a contrast. As God's absence is greater than any known distance, His nearness will "bear the bell" that unifies two in one.

The Parts of the Picture Come Together

Above all else, this poem is a prayer—and certainly a passionate one. It begins with a question that is really a petition to "My Lord, My Love." Contained in this address are the submission, the softness, and the seriousness of "the search." Nothing is held back in the search that spans the sky, but it is also nothing that has been found. It is on this nothingness that the speaker dwells as he gives illustrations of his situation.

First, he contrasts his decay with the "green and gay herbs" and the shining stars that seem to have the way to God's love. Next, he records his efforts in sending forth sighs rooted in his pain, but these efforts were in vain. Having described his situation and recorded his efforts to seek out God, the speaker turns the focus on God. He has more questions. Has God left to "some new fabric mould," and thereby abandoned his old creatures to their sins? Where is the hidden place that conceals God? And then comes the hardest question of all—is all this caused by God's will?

Here the speaker's frustration intensifies. The worse thing is not that the speaker cannot find God: instead, the worse thing is that God wills (or at least seems to) this separation between himself and the speaker. Here there is hopelessness, for God's will cannot be overcome by thought or strength; nor can its "strange distance" be comprehended. The answer is not within the speaker's resources. This is the critical point in the prayer. The speaker has described his painful and fruitless efforts, has inquired into the possible reasons for God's absence, and now realizes that he can do nothing if all this is God's will. With all that in mind, the speaker could sink further into despair and simply give up.

Instead he chooses another path. He renews his petition to his Lord. Rather than languish in the despair of his lack of productivity and of his unanswered questions, instead of dwelling on the insurmountable odds against overcoming God's will, the speaker states his simple plea: "Lord, see my charge (burden), see my case, take these barriers away." And then, as if to remind the Lord of the greatness of the gift of His presence, the speaker mentions the nearness and the unity that comes with that presence. It is a presence only God can bestow—surely that kind of gift could not be withheld. With this concluding appeal—one based on the speaker's opening up to God with praise and yearning—"the search" is placed in God's hands.

Reflections

1. What does the poem have to say about relationship with God?
2. What spiritual direction does it provide?
3. Have you ever "searched" for God? Or, stated another way, have you ever felt separation from God in a manner similar to that portrayed in this poem? If so, how would you describe your feelings during this search? What did you learn from your search?
4. How would you talk to a fellow Christian who is in the throes of a search similar to the one described in this poem? Would this poem assist you in that endeavor? In what way(s)?

Scriptures for further reflection:

Psalm 10:1
Psalm 22:1-2
Song of Songs 3:1-2
Habakkuk 1:2
Matthew 27:46

DENIAL

When my devotions could not pierce
   Thy silent ears;
Then was my heart broken, as was my verse:
  My breast was full of fears
     And disorder: 5

My bent thoughts, like a brittle bow,
   Did fly asunder:
Each took his way; some would to pleasures go,
   Some to the wars and thunder
     Of alarms.   10

As good go anywhere, they say,
   As to benumb
Both knees and heart, in crying night and day,
  Come, come, my God, O come,
     But no hearing.   15

O that thou shouldst give dust a tongue
   To cry to thee,
And then not hear it crying! All day long
  My heart was in my knee,
     But no hearing.   20

Therefore my soul lay out of sight,
   Untuned, unstrung:
My feeble spirit, unable to look right,
  Like a nipped blossom, hung
     Discontented.   25

O cheer and tune my heartless breast,
   Defer no time;
That so thy favors granting my request,
  They and my mind may chime,
     And mend my rhyme.   30

The Big Picture

This poem is about rejection, the feelings associated with the speaker's experience of God's denying him relationship. It is a complaint lamenting the isolation of the speaker. The problem, from the speaker's perspective, is that God no longer hears him. As a consequence, his heart breaks, his "bent thoughts... fly asunder" as his spirit and soul wither. As the poem concludes, the poet turns to God, asking for restoration of relationship.

The Parts of the Picture

The **first stanza** presents the origin of problem. The speaker's feelings of rejection began when his "devotions" (presumably his prayers) failed to "pierce" God's "silent ears." Not only was his heart broken but also was his verse as "fears" and "disorder" filled his breast. Note that the first effect of broken relationship is the broken heart. For Herbert, this is the place where the relationship is tied together. And closely tied to the broken heart is broken verse since his verse flows out of his heart relationship with God. The void created by the broken heart in the breast is now "full of fears and disorder."

One aspect of the disorder is represented by the use of this word in line 5. With this concluding word of the first stanza, the rhyme scheme is broken as the final line is not tied by rhyme to the other four in the stanza. This disorder in the rhyme scheme will continue in the last line of each stanza until the final stanza. In this respect, this poem is another of Herbert's pattern poems in which a pattern in the poem reflects a significant aspect of its meaning. In this poem, the pattern is found in the broken rhyme scheme. As John Wall, Jr., points out, "The lack of harmony between man and God is suggested by the absence of rhyme at the end of each stanza save the last..."[41]

Whereas stanza 1 stated the problem in its inception and described the immediate effect of the brokenness of heart and verse, **stanzas 2-4** intensify the complaint with further description of the effects of the speaker's condition. There are, in stanza 2, the "bent thoughts, like a broken bow" that "fly asunder," each to its own way. **Stanza 3** makes the point that it is as good for these bent thoughts to go anywhere (as they do when they fly asunder as described in stanza 2) as it is for the speaker to " benumb/Both his knees and heart" as he continues to cry to God—"But no hearing." **Stanza 4** further intensifies the complaint in a twofold manner. First, the speaker laments God's cruelty of giving man ("dust") a tongue to call to God and then declining to hear the cry. Second, he contrasts his efforts and God's response. All "day long" he lifts his broken heart prayerfully on bended knee, "But no hearing" there is on God's part.

The "Therefore" that begins **stanza 5** indicates a summation. As a result of the "no hearing" and "silent ears" of God and the consequent broken heart, discordant thoughts, and ineffective prayers of the speaker, his soul is "untuned, unstrung," his spirit "unable to look right," like a "nipped blossom, hung/ Discontented."

74

With stanza 6 the poem takes a new turn. The complaint is finished; now the petition is stated. The poem could have ended in despair, but the speaker, despite all the previous "no hearings" of God, turns again to Him in hope. The request is for renewed relationship, for God to "cheer and tune" the speaker's "heartless breast" as soon as possible so that harmony may be re-established between the speaker's mind and God's favor, thereby mending his rhyme.

The Parts of the Picture Come Together

How does one deal with feelings of being rejected by God? Rather than repressing these feelings or projecting them in anger onto someone other than God, the speaker talks to God. In a lawyer-like fashion, he pleads his case. First, there is the statement of the problem: God's denial of the poet's "devotions." This is followed immediately by a description of the subsequent disorder of the speaker's condition. His despair is evident in the blunt, bold declaration that God is at the root of things gone wrong. There is no praise, no confession of sin, not even a hint of the speaker's searching after some possible failure on his part. Simply put, the speaker is hurt deeply, and God is the problem. The speaker's "devotions" are contrasted to God's "silent ears." The effects are devastating: a broken heart, broken verse, tears, and bent thoughts.

And this is just the beginning. The argument intensifies with further descriptions of the effects of God's denial: thoughts flying asunder and passionate prayer "but no hearing." The climax comes in the accusation of cruelty: God has given the speaker a tongue but there is "no hearing" when that tongue cries out to God. The case has been laid out. A summary is then made with a concise restatement of the poet's condition: his soul is "untuned, unstrung," his spirit "discontented."

Here the speaker could have stopped if he were merely interested in winning an argument. The case has been made. God's creature, in deep devotion, has been torn asunder by God's denial. Pure bitterness would have left the argument there. Complete separation from God would have stopped with the speaker's summary accusation against God. But the speaker does not conclude on that note. He concludes, rather, with a petition, a petition indicating a remnant of relationship and a deep desire for restored relationship. The speaker has made clear that the problem is with God, and he concludes by making it even clearer that the answer is in God. Finally, then, the poem is not a declaration of defiance and accusation, although it is laden with those elements. Finally, the speaker submits to the only One capable of giving new life, new "chime," new "rhyme." After the speaker has had his say, after the depths of his despair have been fully expressed, the speaker makes his move toward God, lifting his plea to God, casting his lot with God, anticipating renewal of relationship with God. The parts have come together—the statement and the effects of the problem, the accumulation of evidence of the poet's despair, and finally the petition for renewal of relationship. To God the speaker has pleaded his case, and finally to God he gives himself.

Reflections

1. What does the poem have to say about relationship with God?
2. What spiritual direction does it provide?
3. Have you, like the speaker, felt as if you could not connect with God? How did you handle your feelings? From your reading of this poem, what do you think this poet would want you to do in that situation?
4. If you had a friend who felt abandoned by God, in what way might this poem be helpful to you in talking with that friend?

Scriptures for further reflection:

Psalm 44:23-26
Psalm 83:1
Psalm 88:13-14
Jeremiah 15:18; and 17:14

CHURCH LOCK AND KEY

I know it is my sin, which locks thine ears,
                And binds thy hands,
Out-crying my requests, drowning my tears;
Or else the chillness of my faint demands.

But as cold hands are angry with the fire,   5
                And mend it still;
So I do lay the want of my desire,
Not on my sins, or coldness, but thy will.

Yet hear, O God, only for his blood's sake
                Which pleads for me: 10
For though sins plead too, yet like stones they make
His blood's sweet current much more loud to be.

The Big Picture

As its title indicates, the poem is about a lock and a key. The "lock" is the poet's sin which separates him from God, "locking" God's ears and "binding" God's hands and thereby negating God's response to the speaker's requests and tears. The "key" is Christ's blood "which pleads" for the poet. The poem, therefore, is simply concerned with the key (Christ's blood) unlocking the lock (the effects of the poet's sins). In short, it is a prayer of confession, surrender, and petition.

The Parts of the Picture

Stanza 1. The speaker confesses that his sin separates him from God or else it is "the chillness of my faint demands" (probably a reference to the coldness and faintness that have developed in the poet in his relationship with God). The result is the locking of God's ears, the binding of His hands, and the nullifying of the speaker's requests and tears.

Stanza 2. He compares himself to cold hands that are "angry with the fire" ("angry" perhaps because they are an inflamed "angry red" from coldness or because the fire is too slow in warming them, or both) but still tend to it. Like the cold hands, the speaker (despite his anger with God) persists and lays his desire on God's will.

Stanza 3. The speaker's petition is for God to hear his prayer for the sake of Christ who "pleads for" him. The speaker's sins plead, also. As Christ's "sweet current" rushes through these sins, it is like a current rushing over and around stones, thereby increasing the loud sound like a rushing torrent.

The Parts of the Picture Come Together

If, as is commonly thought by Christians, sin involves separation from God, one may safely say that this poem begins with sin. With his choice of verbs ("locks" and "binds"), nouns ("sin," "tears," and "chillness"), and participles ("outcrying" and "drowning"), the speaker paints a graphic picture of the despair of separation from God. Because of the speaker's sin, God's ears are locked and His hands are bound. Indeed the sin is so powerful that communication is impossible as the sin "outcries" the speaker's requests and drowns his tears. The speaker begins where he should as a Christian—he confesses that all this is true.

But the speaker does not stop with mere confession—to do so for an extended time would be to choose to dwell in paralyzing self-pity. Instead, the speaker moves outside himself. The intensity of the feelings remains (as reflected in the imagery of cold hands, anger, and fire), but it heads in a positive direction—towards God! The speaker's desire is to lay all on God's will. The poem began with separation—now it has reached surrender.

And there is further movement. The speaker has confessed, he has surrendered, and now in the final stanza, he intensifies his petition by focusing on the blood of Christ "which pleads for me." For relief to come, for new life to emerge, more that confession and surrender are necessary. Confession and surrender come from man, but forgiveness comes only from God. The blood of Christ is, therefore, necessary for it is the only key that can open the way to God.

In the final two lines, the speaker creates a climactic image by mixing the blood of Christ and the speaker's sins. This brings together the "lock" and "key." It is an image of blood running like a current through rocks resulting in the current (Christ's blood) being made louder by its washing against the rocks (the speaker's sins). This image captures the essence of the speaker's petition. It is only the washing of the speaker's sins by the blood of Christ that can heighten the sound of the plea for forgiveness and thereby bring this plea to God and unlock the bondage of separation.

Reflections

1. What does the poem have to say about relationship with God?
2. What spiritual direction does it provide?
3. Have there been times when you have felt "locked in" or separated from God? How would you describe your feelings during those times? Did they resemble in any way the feelings manifested by the speaker in this poem?
4. What is your response to how the speaker dealt with his situation as described in stanza 1 in this poem?

Scriptures for further reflection:

Matthew 26:27-28
John 1:29
Romans 3:25
Epheslans 1:7
I John 1:7

NOTES

PETITION

*M*any of Herbert's poems are prayers of petition. Some of them are found under other topics in this work. The six poems arranged under this topic provide examples of ways in which Herbert approached God with his petitions. *Nature* is a confession within a petition as the speaker confesses his heart "full of rebellion" while petitioning God to "smooth his rugged heart." *Gratefulness* is another confession within a petition as the speaker confesses ungratefulness while petitioning for a grateful heart. *Easter Wings* is praise within a petition as the speaker praises the Resurrection power of God while petitioning God to let him also rise and combine with Christ in His victory. *Employment* is a lament within a petition as the speaker laments his woeful state of languishing without employment as he petitions God to have a place in His "great chain." *Discipline* is a well-reasoned argument petitioning God to discipline the speaker in a certain manner. Finally, *The Elixir* is a petition for teaching so that the speaker may become aware of the transforming power of God in all things.

NATURE

Full of rebellion, I would die,
Or fight, or travel, or deny
That thou hast ought to do with me.
$\qquad$ O tame my heart;
$\qquad$ It is thy highest art $\qquad$ 5
To captivate strong holds to thee.

If thou shalt let this venom lurk,
And in suggestions fume and work,
My soul will turn to bubbles straight,
$\qquad$ And thence by kind $\qquad$ 10
$\qquad$ Vanish into a wind,
Making thy workmanship deceit.

O smooth my rugged heart, and there
Engrave thy reverend Law and fear;
Or make a new one, since the old $\qquad$ 15
$\qquad$ Is sapless grown,
$\qquad$ And a much fitter stone
To hide my dust, then thee to hold.

The Big Picture

The poem is primarily a prayer of petition, but first it is a confession. The poem presents the speaker's "rebellion," the struggle within his "rugged heart." Authentically, with utmost transparency, the poet reveals the venom lurking in his nature and then presses his pleas to God to transform his heart. It is a poem with rebellion and humility, desperation and confidence, threat and dependence, self-centeredness and submission. Most importantly, it is a plea for God's help, for a renewal of the poet's heart.

The Parts of the Picture

Divisions. The poem's three stanzas reflect its main divisions. Within the **first stanza** are two subdivisions. The first three lines state forcefully the speaker's rebellious state, and then in lines 4-6 the tone and substance shift suddenly to a plea and a statement about God's ability to deal with his state. The **second stanza** intensifies with a series of vivid images conveying what will happen to him if God allows his current state to continue. With the **third stanza**, the tone softens to a more subtle plea, but the petition remains firm and even forceful as the plea is expanded to the need for a new heart.

Biblical Allusions. The second and climactic plea in the poem is for a heart engraved with "thy reverend law and fear" (line 14) or for a new heart (lines 15-18). This is similar to many biblical allusions to God's ability to remake man's heart (see especially Psalm 51:10, Ezekiel 36:26, and Jeremiah 31:33).

The Parts of the Picture Come Together

The intensity of the inner struggle of the speaker is reflected throughout the poem in the rather sudden shifts from rebellion, to plea, to a severe description of what will happen if God does not act, and finally to another plea.

The poem begins with "full" rebellion, as reflected in the force of the verbs in the first three lines: "die," "fight," "travel," and "deny." Somewhat ironically the rebellion is connected to the speaker's unworthiness (line 3) rather than to something God has done. Although the plea that follows in lines 4-6 also reflects intensity, the tone shifts to humility and to confidence in God's ability to take redemptive action. Thus, the first movement of the poem clearly reflects that the speaker is torn: full of rebellion but also in need of being tamed.

The next movement (lines 6-12) verges on a threat. Indeed, it is a threat but one that is really an expansion of the speaker's plea for God to tame his heart. This threat/plea presents vivid images of what will happen if God does not act. The desperate state of the speaker has reached its climax.

The final movement is another plea. It is a plea that retains the intensity of what has gone before, but a softer, more subtle tone emerges as the theme of the speaker's unworthiness returns and the extent of his need is clarified. Now the plea is not only to "smooth" his "rugged" heart but to engrave it with God's Law and the reverent fear of God. But probably more is needed, and that more is a new heart since his old one is "much fitter...to hide my dust" than to hold God.

The movements are multifaceted and unpredictable, but there is also a unity that ties the movements together. The references in each stanza to "heart" (line 4), "soul" (line 9), and "heart" (line 13) give the poem a unifying focus while allowing the struggle itself to take its natural shifts. And God is at the center of it all. Hence, there is subtle unity within the upheaval of the struggle. Such is the nature of the heart and soul struggling with God.

Reflections

1. What does the poem say about relationship with God?
2. What spiritual direction does it provide?
3. One of the appealing things about the prayer of this poem is its honesty with God. Does the poem encourage you to vent with utmost honesty your deepest feelings to God?
4. How has struggle with God manifested itself in your journey with Him? Is the poem helpful—

    a. in coming to a better understanding of your struggle; and/or

    b. in dealing with the frustrations that often are part of that struggle?
5. The speaker finds himself simultaneously in rebellion with God but also dependent on Him to resolve the struggle. Have you found yourself in a similar situation?

Scriptures for further reflection:

Psalm 51:10
Jeremiah 31:33
Ezekiel 36:26
Matthew 22:36-38
Romans 7:14-25

GRATEFULNESS

Thou that hast given so much to me,
Give one thing more, a grateful heart.
See how thy beggar works on thee
        By art.

He makes thy gifts occasion more,   5
And says, If he in this be crossed,
All thou hast given him heretofore
        Is lost.

But thou didst reckon, when at first
Thy word our hearts and hands did crave,   10
What it would come to at the worst
        To save.

Perpetual knockings at thy door,
Tears sullying thy transparent rooms,
Gift upon gift, much would have more,   15
        And comes.

This notwithstanding, thou wentst on,
And didst allow us all our noise:
Nay, thou hast made a sigh and groan
        Thy joys.   20

Not that thou hast not still above
Much better tunes, then groans can make;
But that these country-airs thy love
        Did take.

Wherefore I cry, and cry again;   25
And in no quiet canst thou be,
Till I a thankful heart obtain
        Of thee:

Not thankful, when it pleaseth me;
As if thy blessings had spare days: 30
But such a heart, whose pulse may be
             Thy praise.

The Big Picture

This is a poem of contrasts. There is the picture of the selfish speaker, with his unbounded desire for God to give to him unceasingly. There is God who, despite man's lack of gratefulness, continues to love him. And there is the speaker who, though self-centered to the core, confesses and laments his sin. But, what is most important, the poem is a petition to God by the speaker for one thing more—a grateful heart.

The Parts of the Picture

Stanzas 1- 2. These two stanzas state the basic request of the speaker and introduce his ungratefulness. Lines 1 and 2 contain the request for a grateful heart, the "one thing more" the speaker desires. Line 3 begins the explanation for the need for such a heart. Through the end of stanza 2, the speaker ("thy beggar") is portrayed as one who, "by art," works on God. This "art" is a form of bribery. The speaker "makes" or compels God's gifts to become the "occasion" for more gifts, and tells God that, if God crosses him and denies a gift, the value of the previous gifts will be lost.

Stanzas 3-6. The focus shifts from the speaker to God. "At first" (or "in the beginning") when God's word (as in John 1:1, "in the beginning was the Word") "craved" (or wanted to bring forth) mankind's "hearts and hands," God knew that the creation of man would "come to at the worst." Or do lines 9b and 10 mean that in the beginning when mankind did crave or desire God's word, God knew that it would come to at the worse? In other words, is "Thy word" or "our hearts and hands" the subject of line 10? Or is this a deliberate ambiguity by Herbert so that the line could be read both ways? Helen Wilcox points out that this line is "a perfectly ambivalent line".[42] At any rate, from the beginning God knew it would come to the worst in order to save man and, as described in stanza 4, the "worst" of man "comes" (notice the connection between "come" in line 11 and "comes" in line 16). This "worst" consists of man's ceaseless knocking, his tears "sullying" God's dwelling place (with "transparent rooms"), and God's outpouring of gifts failing to satisfy man. In short, what God knew it would "come to," to that it "comes." As stanza 5 points out, however, God permitted man's "noise" and even found joy in it. And although God can listen to "better tunes" than man's groans, God's love "did take" to (or found favor in) the "country airs" or musical notes of man (stanza 6). This is a truly gracious God.

Stanzas 7 and 8. The focus shifts back to the speaker. He will persevere in his petition. God will have "no quiet" until the speaker receives a grateful heart (stanza 7).

As the speaker concludes, he clarifies further his request. The grateful heart he desires is not one that is grateful only when the speaker is pleased. Since God's blessings have no "spare days," the speaker's desire is for a heart whose very pulse consists of praising God (stanza 8.)

The Parts of the Picture Come Together

A mixture of confession, petition, and praise drives this poem. First stated is the core petition for a grateful heart. Then comes the first statement of confession of the speaker's "art" of being a "beggar" with unrelenting self-centered requests of God. In short, the poem begins (stanzas 1 and 2) with a petition for gratefulness based on a confession of ungratefulness.

Then the poem shifts (stanzas 3-6) to praise with an undercurrent of continuing confession. Great is God's faithfulness despite mankind's "perpetual knockings," "noise," "tears sullying," and "groans." The contrast of God and man is stark. Here is the backbone of the poem. In God things hold together. It is God who holds together the relationship with man despite man's self-absorption. It is God who transforms man's "sigh and groan" into His joy. It is God who, despite having "better tunes" "above," lovingly accepts man's "country airs." It is to this God that the speaker confesses and cries for a grateful heart.

In the closing two stanzas, the poem shifts back to the speaker with a forceful restatement of his petition for a grateful heart. Here is petition with an undertone of a serious, but also somewhat playful, threat reflecting the speaker's desperate state—God will "in no quiet...be" until the speaker has a "thankful heart," a heart whose very pulse praises God in all things, pleasing or unpleasing.

The poem, therefore, moves from petition and confession to God to praise of God and concludes with more petition. It is a portrayal of the speaker going beyond the sin of self-centeredness by confessing that sin. But greater than the confession is the confidence in God. It is a confidence proven by the past and a confidence hopeful for the future—a future full of gratefulness, Thanks be to God!

Reflections

1. What does this poem have to say about relationship with God?
2. What spiritual direction does it provide?
3. How would you evaluate your prayer life? Is it mostly centered on self? Or is it God-centered? Or otherwise? How does your prayer life reflect your relationship with God?
4. If you had only "one thing more" to ask of God, what would it be? Why?

Scriptures for further reflection:

Psalm 119:35-37   Hebrews 10:22-23

EASTER WINGS

Lord, who created man in wealth and store,
Though foolishly he lost the same,
Decaying more and more,
Till he became
Most poor: 5
With thee
O let me rise
As larks, harmoniously,
And sing this day thy victories:
Then shall the fall further the flight in me.   10

My tender age in sorrow did begin:
And still with sicknesses and shame
Thou didst so punish sin,
That I became
Most thin.   15
With thee
Let me combine
And feel this day thy victory:
For, if I imp my wing on thine,
Affliction shall advance the flight in me.   20

The Big Picture

This poem is a prayer containing assorted elements: praise, confession, petition, admission of defeat, and anticipation of victory. It is a prayer about the general state of mankind and the particular state of the speaker. It is a prayer that sees the whole of Christian life as it deals with loss, decay, affliction, descent, sorrow, and sin alongside harmony, victory, ascent, advancement, and dependence. Above all, it is a petition to partake in the power of Easter wings to give flight to the fallen.

The Parts of the Picture

This is a pattern poem in that its shape reflects aspects of its meaning. The shape of the lines are like the movement of wings in flight and reflect the fall and rise of the lark's flight and also of the fall of man and the rise of the Easter event.

Stanza 1. Here the subject is mankind and the fall. After the descent from the creation through the fall to "most poor" at the mid-point of the stanza in line 5, the thoughts ascend with the speaker's petition to rise victoriously with the Lord on Easter. Finally, the opposites of fall and flight are united and reconciled as the stanza closes.

Stanza 2. The focus shifts to the particular situation of the speaker as sin and punishment diminish him to "most thin" in line 15. At that point, as at the mid-point in stanza 1, the lines begin to expand with the speaker's petition to combine with the Lord in victory "this day." And as in the last line of stanza 1, opposites (affliction and advancement) are united and reconciled at the fullest point of expansion.

Biblical allusions. In the speaker's petitioning of the Lord for a renewal of strength, there are two possible biblical allusions: Isaiah 40:31 and Malachi 4:2.

Rhyme Scheme. This is used both to divide thought within each stanza and to intertwine the two stanzas. First, the rhyme schemes reflect the subdivisions within the stanzas. *ababa, cdcdc,* for stanza 1 and *ebebe, cfcfc,* for stanza 2. Secondly, the rhyme schemes connect the two stanzas. There are interlocking rhymes in lines 2 and 12, 4 and 14, 6 and 16, 8 and 18, and 10 and 20. This interlocking by rhyme is re-enforced in three of these cases by a repetition of the same words: "became" in lines 4 and 14; "thee" in lines 6 and 16; and "me" in lines 10 and 20.

The Parts of the Picture Come Together

In the Easter event, God moved dramatically from negative to positive, from death to life. Note this movement in the poem. Each stanza compresses in shape as it descends in spirit and then expands and rises. Mankind loses (line 2) but God's power can raise him to victory (lines 7 and 9). The poet is impoverished (line 15) but also knows the power of combining with Christ's wing (line 19). This movement is portrayed boldly in the climactic last lines of each stanza with "fall" furthering "flight" (line 10) and "affliction" advancing "flight" (line 20).

For the speaker of this poem, Easter is much more than an event in the past. It is even more than the celebration of such an event. As indicated by the prominence of the petitions in lines 6-10 and 16-20 (half of the poem is petition), the speaker desires for himself the power of the Easter experience. At the heart of the prayer, therefore, is a petition for a personal Easter event to "sing this day" (line 9) and to "feel this day" (line 18). The speaker knows decay (line 3) and poverty (line 5); but he desires flight (lines 7 and 10), song (line 9), and victory (line 9). He knows sorrow, sickness, shame (lines 11 and 12), and frailty (line 15); but he desires to combine with Christ (lines 16-17) and feel His victory (line 18).

What is the way to this victory? The victories pronounced in lines 9 and 18 are Christ's, the victory of Easter. The way to victory, therefore, is to combine with Christ (lines 16-18). This union is portrayed vividly in line 19—"If I imp my wing on thine." To "imp" is to repair a damaged wing by engrafting feathers onto it. In short, the speaker's brokenness can be made whole in his union with Christ who engrafts the power of Easter wings. This "combining" with Christ comes to a climax in the last line of the poem. Affliction, the speaker says, can advance his flight. Not only can his afflictions do this, but, more importantly, Christ's can. And even more importantly, the combination of the two afflictions is the key to the flight of Easter wings. For the speaker, therefore, in a most personal way, the power of Easter triumphantly unites the opposites of affliction and flight as it brings forth newness of life. And in a most personal way, the speaker petitions God to partake in this resurrection power.

Reflections

Obviously, for Christians, so much hinges on the event of Easter. It is the triumphant culmination of the Incarnation. It is the source of hope for sharing in God's victory. God's work and our faith are incomplete without it. As the apostle Paul points out, "if Christ be not raised, your faith is vain" (I Cor. 15:17). So to say that Christians rejoice in the happening of Easter is an understatement. One challenge for us, however, is to go beyond the concept of Easter as only a happening of the past. If Easter is to bring its power to our personal lives, there must be an experiential as well as historical dimension to it. "Easter Wings" gives us Herbert's petition for that experiential dimension of Easter. A potentially important function of the poem is the "experiential bridge" to Easter that it can be for us. Considering the following questions may be helpful in this regard:

1. What does the poem have to say about relationship with God?
2. What spiritual direction does it provide?
3. How would you describe the poem? As a powerful personal experience to which you can (or cannot) relate? As a source of encouragement? Otherwise?
4. Does it add to, affirm, or re-shape your view of Easter?
5. If you were writing your thoughts about Easter, how would they be similar to and/or different from those expressed in this poem?
6. "Easter is an encounter with the Risen Lord," it was once said. Would you agree? Is the poem helpful as you consider this?

Scriptures for further reflection:

Exodus 15:1-18	I Corinthians 15:54-58
Isaiah 40:31	Job 19:25-27
Luke 24:36-43	Revelation 20:6
John 11:25	Philippians 3:10

EMPLOYMENT (I)

If as a flower doth spread and die,
  Thou wouldst extend me to some good,
Before I were by frosts extremity
            Nipped in the bud;

The sweetness and the praise were thine;   5
  But the extension and the room,
Which in thy garland I should fill, were mine
            At thy great doom.

For as thou dost impart thy grace,
  The greater shall our glory be.   10
The measure of our joys is in this place,
            The stuff with thee.

Let me not languish then, and spend
  A life as barren to thy praise,
As is the dust, to which that life doth tend,   15
            But with delays.

All things are busy; only I
  Neither bring honey with the bees,
Nor flowers to make that, nor the husbandry
            To water these.   20

I am no link of thy great chain,
  But all my company is a weed.
Lord place me in thy consort; give one strain
            To my poor reed.

The Big Picture

This poem is a petition in the form of a lament. It is a prayer by one who feels he has no meaningful work. It is a petition for God to give the speaker "some good" so that, like "all things," he may be "busy." It is an expression of one who feels "barren" of God's praise. It is a plea for God to find him a place in his "consort." The poem is not dated, and the exact circumstances of Herbert's life cannot be determined, although it is clear that Herbert went through periods, sometimes extended, of vocational uncertainty and even despair. This poem is surely a product of one of those periods. The poem thereby reflects another dimension of Herbert's relationship with God as he reaches out to Him in this dark time.

The Parts of the Picture

Stanza 1. The speaker uses the analogy to a flower to state his plea. As a flower spreads (or blooms) before it dies, may it be that God would "extend" the speaker "to some good" before he is "nipped in the bud."

Stanzas 2 and 3. While continuing to advance his plea, the speaker turns the focus away from himself and toward God. To God goes the "sweetness and praise," it is God's grace that determines mankind's glory, although "the measure of our joys" or a limited amount of joy is our earth, the substantial "stuff" lies with God. In contrast, the poet's place is merely the "extension and room" that he has, like a flower, in God's garland at God's "great doom" or last judgment.

In Stanzas 4 and 5, the speaker furthers his plea by recasting the focus upon himself. The plea was first stated positively in stanza 1, using the analogy of a flower blooming. Now in stanza 4, the plea is stated negatively ("let me not languish") using images of dust and barrenness. In stanza 5, the plea is restated in a third way. He contrasts his state to the fact that "all things are busy"—the bees with their honey, the flowers, and those engaged in husbandry or cultivation of the flowers.

The **final stanza** brings together several images. First, the speaker states his condition. He is not a part of God's great chain of being; rather, he is in the company of a weed serving no good purpose. Then, again he makes his plea. He wants to be a part, a small part ("one strain"), of a consort of musicians performing for God.

The Parts of the Picture Come Together

The poem captures a moment of great importance in Christian spirituality—a moment of despair. How a Christian responds to this feeling is critical to his relationship with God. Here the speaker reaches out to God, following the biblical tradition of the laments in the Psalms, the confessions of Jeremiah, and the prayers of Jesus at Gethsemane and on the Cross.

The speaker's plea is a humble one. Neither fame nor any other kind of prominence is sought. His plea, most simply put, is to be as useful as a flower, as busy as a bee, as efficient as one musician in the consort of others. He, like everyman, does not want to languish. He merely wants to be engaged in meaningful activity. He is careful not to base his plea on his own merit. Furthermore, the speaker makes clear his understanding that God's grace is the source of all mankind's glory and that with God is the "stuff" of joy.

It is indeed a simple, straightforward, heartfelt, humble plea with no strings attached. And, unfortunately, as is often the case with laments, no answer comes—only the condition is described and the plea made. Perhaps this reaching out to God is all that can be done at a time such as that described in the poem. Perhaps the expression of these feelings is enough—at least for the time being. After all, this is no small achievement. Such expression is simply a part of the journey, a part of the working out of our salvation. Surely the "great cloud of witnesses" would applaud the speaker's effort.

Reflections

1. What does the poem have to say about relationship to God?
2. What spiritual direction does it provide?
3. How do you handle times of distress such as the one described in this poem?
4. What is there to say to God about your work? And how should you say it?

Scriptures for further reflection:

Psalm 31:1-5
Psalm 102:1-2 and 11
Psalm 143:7-8
Jeremiah 29:11-13
John 15:2

DISCIPLINE

Throw away thy rod,
Throw away thy wrath:
   O my God,
Take the gentle path.

For my heart's desire   5
Unto thine is bent:
   I aspire
To a full consent.

Not a word or look
I affect to own,   10
   But by book,
And thy book alone.

Though I fail, I weep:
Though I halt in pace,
   Yet I creep   15
To the throne of grace.

Then let wrath remove;
Love will do the deed:
   For with love
Stony hearts will bleed.   20

Love is a swift of foot;
Love's a man of war,
   And can shoot,
And can hit from far.

Who can scape his bow?   25
That which wrought on thee,
   Brought thee low,
Needs must work on me.

Throw away thy rod;
Though man frailties hath,
        Thou art God:
Throw away thy wrath.

        30

The Big Picture

This is a humble but persistent plea to God to "throw away thy wrath." Only the speaker and God are subjects of concern. Nothing else and no one else are mentioned. The issue is the manner by which God will discipline the speaker. There is not even a hint about why the discipline is needed. The poem is pure petition, a carefully constructed argument designed to convince God to discipline the speaker with "the gentle path" of love.

The Parts of the Picture

Stanza 1. The essence of the petition to God is stated: "throw away thy rod" and "take the gentle path" in the matter of disciplining the speaker.

Stanzas 2-4. The first part of the speaker's argument for "the gentle path" of discipline is grounded in himself. Though he fails, weeps, and halts, and though he creeps to the "throne of Grace," the speaker's "heart's desire" is just, and he owns only God's book.

Stanzas 5-7. The second part of the speaker's argument is focused on the nature and sufficiency of God's love to accomplish the task. Love can conquer hearts, it is a swift man of war, and it even brought God "low" (possibly an allusion to John 3:16 and other scriptures which speak of the cost of God's love in redeeming mankind).

Stanza 8. The poem comes full circle with a plea that echoes the first stanza and also echoes Hosea 11:9.

The Parts of the Picture Come Together

How does a person talk to God about the nature of the discipline that God should administer to the person? Here the speaker uses a direct, humble, intimate approach. But although humble (stanza 4 and lines 30-31) and deeply respectful (lines 3 and 31), the speaker approaches God with a clear and persistent purpose to persuade.

For the speaker, it is perfectly clear what God is to do: "Take the gentle path." And he argues forthrightly why God should take that path: the speaker's heart (stanza 2) and actions (stanza 3 and 4) are ripe for grace. And there is no doubt about the sufficiency of love to accomplish the task. Indeed, it is a declaration of God's very nature on which the final appeal is made: "Thou art God."

But it is more than the nature of God alone that makes this poem what it is. And the poem is more than the reverent but unrelenting argumentative tone of the speaker. Overriding and tying together these aspects of the poem is the speaker's confidence in his relationship with God.

With God, the speaker is at ease. He is straightforward and bold; he presses his argument without apology. He goes to the main point and stays with it. There is no wavering. The choice and arrangement of the language reflects the discipline of the speaker as he petitions for discipline. As Joseph Summers points out, the language of the poem "imitates the title... and the result is a bareness of statement rare in English poetry."[45] And yet there is, interwoven in all of this, a clear sense of intimacy with, reverence for, and dependence on God. The speaker needs God's love; and he is emboldened to ask for it with no equivocation. It is indeed a relationship of confidence marked by the directness of simplicity and the deep richness of love.

Reflections

1. What does the poem have to say about relationship with God?
2. What spiritual direction does it provide?
3. How do you usually think of God's disciplining His people?
4. Do you agree with the speaker in his argument that God should discipline with love? Or does it depend on the circumstances?
5. Is the concept of God disciplining us with love an unfamiliar or difficult concept for you? What does it mean? Does it appeal to you? Or do you have problems with it?
6. Can you imagine yourself petitioning God for discipline of a certain kind? For what kind of discipline would you petition, and how would you present your plea?

Scriptures for further reflection:
Psalm 6:1-4
Isaiah 12:1-2
Hosea 11:8-9
John 8:1-12
Hebrews 4:16

THE ELIXIR

Teach me, my God and King,
    In all things thee to see,
And what I do in any thing,
    To do it as for thee:

Not rudely, as a beast,   5
    To run into an action;
But still to make thee prepossessed,
    And give it his perfection.

A man that looks on glass,
    On it may stay his eye;   10
Or if he pleaseth, through it pass,
    And then the heaven espy.

All may of thee partake:
    Nothing can be so mean,
Which with his tincture (for thy sake)   15
    Will not grow bright and clean.

A servant with this cause
    Makes drudgery divine:
Who sweeps a room, as for thy laws,
    Makes that and the action fine.   20

This is the famous stone
    That turneth all to gold:
For that which God doth touch and own
    Cannot for less be told.

The Big Picture

This poem is a petition that God will teach the speaker to see God in all things. In making this petition, the speaker praises God's power to transform into gold all things offered to Him. All this is a call to the reader to approach things with the right attitude of allowing God to be foremost. It is a call to act in a way that gives God priority and a foremost claim. If that is done, the "mean" or lowest will grow "bright and clean, and a servant sweeping a room will make "drudgeries divine."

The Parts of the Picture

The Title. *Elixir* usually refers to a magical or medicinal substance. In this poem, elixir is a reference to a stone (the "famous stone" of line 21) claimed to have the powers to turn metals into gold.

Stanzas 1-2. The poem begins as a prayer of petition. The request is for teaching. It is a plea that God empower the speaker to act in all things for God. The request is completed in the second stanza as the speaker prays that he will not act "rudely, as a beast," but that he will always ("still") give God priority ("prepossessed") so as to give the action its ("his") perfection.

Stanza 3. The speaker gives an illustration. A man who keeps his eye on only glass sees only the glass. But if he looks through the glass, then he can see heaven or see God.

Stanza 4. The theme is restated. Nothing is so small (or "mean") that it does not partake of God. A thing's tincture ("his" means "its" as in line 8 and refers to the "action" in line 6) or alchemical essence (as in the elixir stone) can grow bright and clean for God's sake.

Stanza 5. Another illustration is provided. A servant "with this clause" (i.e., the "for thy sake" of line 15) can make "divine" the drudgery of sweeping a room if done for God's laws.

Stanza 6. The "famous stone," the elixir or philosopher's stone, turns all to gold. So, too, whatever God "doth touch" and "own" cannot be counted (or "told") as less than gold.

The Parts of the Picture Come Together

Louis Martz observes that in Herbert's poetry there is a "meditative practice" that Martz describes as "argumentative evolution." It is a way of developing the thought within a poem in three stages: "first compose the problem, then analyze its parts, and end with resolutions and petitions in colloquy with God."[48] Indeed, one of the appealing aspects of Herbert is his ability to move through these stages (problem, analysis, and resolution) while combining creative poetic technique with profound theological insight. The reader can come to expect this of Herbert.

But, as with any noteworthy poet, Herbert is not subject to being reduced to a certain formulaic style. To be sure, his creativity is not limited by any particular way of developing thought. *The Elixir* is an example. This poem lacks the systematic movement from problem to analysis to resolution. Instead, there is a statement of the theme or resolution at the beginning, followed by development through restatement and illustration.

The first two stanzas clearly present a petition to God for teaching. The speaker desires to see God in all things and to do all things for God. Contrast is used. Rather than rudely rushing into action "as a beast" (i.e., as a bull in a china closet), the speaker desires always to give God priority. Then comes the development of this idea by an example. When looking upon a glass, a person may see only the glass, or he may see through it to God. The seeing through the glass to God (rather than seeing only the glass) illustrates the speaker's request in line 1 to always see God first and in lines 7-8 to give God priority.

Then (in stanza 4) the speaker develops his request by universalizing it. "All," no matter how "mean" or small, may partake of God. "Nothing" can be so "mean" that its "tincture" or essence cannot grow "bright and clean" if offered for God's sake. A specific example follows with the image of a servant making "drudgeries divine" by following God's laws in his actions.

The climax comes in the summary in the final stanza. The reason for the desire to see God in all things and do all things for God, as stated in the first stanza, is now made clear. God, like the famous elixir stone, has the power of transforming "all to gold" with His touch.

This is Herbert's version of Brother Lawrence's "practice of the presence of God" or finding God in all things. It is the doing of all things for God. It is the losing of self and of the seeking and finding of God. It can be done by all, especially in the small things of seeing through a glass or sweeping a room. And in the experience of God in all things, in the experience of God touching and owning something, there is the experience of God's transforming power.

Reflections

1. What does the poem have to say about relationship with God?
2. What spiritual direction does it provide?
3. The poem speaks of finding God in all things, of experiencing God's transforming power, of giving priority to God in all things. Do you find yourself inclined to do these things or are you more like one who, as portrayed in stanza 2, runs "rudely, as a beast...into an action"? Or is there another way in which you would describe yourself?
4. Have you known people who are able to live consistently in the manner desired by the speaker in this poem—people who find God and experience His transforming power in things small or large? What is their secret?
5. In what ways are you an obstacle to God using you as his agent, as described in the poem?

Scriptures for further reflection:
Psalm 16:11
Romans 8:28
Philippians 4:11-13

PRAISE

*A*lthough George Herbert definitely experienced dark times in his relationship with God (for examples, see *The Search* and *Denial*), God was Herbert's ultimate joy and delight. Examples of that joy and delight are seen in these poems of praise. *Praise (II)* is pure praise. *The Call* could well be placed under the topic Petition, but it is placed here because most of the poem describes the reasons for the speaker's call for Jesus to come to him.

PRAISE (II)

King of Glory, King of Peace,
          I will love thee:
And that love may never cease,
          I will move thee.

Thou hast granted my request,   5
          Thou hast heard me:
Thou didst note my working breast,
          Thou hast spared me.

Wherefore with my utmost art
          I will sing thee,   10
And the cream of all my heart
          I will bring thee.

Though my sins against me cried,
          Thou didst clear me;
And alone, when they replied,   15
          Thou didst hear me.

Seven whole days, not one in seven,
          I will praise thee.
In my heart, though not in heaven,
          I can raise thee.   20

Thou grewest soft and moist with tears,
          Thou relentedst:
And when Justice called for fears,
          Thou dissentedst.

Small it is, in this poor sort   25
          To enroll thee:
Even eternity is too short
          To extol thee.

The Big Picture

In its weaving together of praise and descriptions of the Lord's actions, this poem resembles Psalm 116. The poem alternates with a declaration in one stanza of how the speaker will praise the Lord, followed by a stanza that describes how the Lord has acted in the speaker's life. Through this interweaving of the speaker's praise and God's saving actions, the poem embodies the bonding of the speaker and God.

The Parts of the Picture

Structure. The arrangement of the first 6 stanzas reflects the "I-Thou" relationship of the speaker and God. Stanzas 1, 3, and 5 proclaim the praises made by "I." Stanzas 2, 4, and 6 describe the praiseworthy acts of "Thou." The poem is encased with an eternal note as it begins with "never cease" and ends with a reference to "eternity." Internally the stanzas are bound together with alternating lines that rhyme. All of this creates a structure as tightly bound together as is the relationship that it describes.

Stanzas 1, 3, and 5. The verbs in these stanzas indicate the nature of the praise: "love," "move," "sing," "bring," "praise," and "raise." Stanza 1 is centered on never-ending love; stanza 3 focuses on the highest expression of praise ("my utmost art" and "the cream of all my heart"); and stanza 5 expresses the continuity and the uplifting of the praise. All of this combines to create a superlative, personal, intense, and continuing form of praise.

Stanzas 2, 4, and 6. The verbs in these stanzas are key to understanding the nature of God's actions in the speaker's life. God has heard and granted a request, noticed workings, spared life, cleared sins, shed tears, and overrode Justice with grace. Indeed, great is the faithfulness of God.

Stanza 7. Here "I" and "Thou" come together. The "I-speaker" is the "poor sort" whose "enrolling" or celebrating is small. The "thee-God" is the one who could not be extolled adequately even with all the time of eternity.

The Parts of the Picture Come Together

Unlike many of Herbert's other poems, this poem does not present a problem and work toward a resolution, or develop an idea sequentially, or tell a story chronologically. Rather, like a psalm intended to be read aloud responsively, it develops an idea through the alternating of praise and a description of the cause of the praise. In this way, the one praising and the One praised are brought and bound together. In short, the poem itself is the working out of the relationship involved.

This is true with one important exception: the last stanza where the one praising and the One praised are contrasted. As if there were some danger in portraying the praise as adequate for the One praised, the speaker concludes by making clear the great difference in the "I" and the "Thee" of the poem. "I" is dwarfed by "Thee." "I" is "small," a "poor sort"; "thee" is too great to be reduced to praise. Although "I" and "Thee" have been given equal time up to this final stanza, and although this "equal time" certainly has furthered the binding together of these two, the ending makes abundantly clear that the poem is "Praise" of "Thou."

Reflections

1. What does this poem have to say about relationship with God?
2. What spiritual direction does it provide?
3. If you were to write a poem of praise to God, what would you praise and how would you arrange the material? Why?
4. How much of your prayer life is praise? What place should praise have in your prayer life - the most important place, the least, or something else? Does it depend on the circumstances? Why and how?

Scriptures for further reflection:

Psalms 145-150
Luke 1:46-55

THE CALL

Come, my Way, my Truth, my Life:
Such a Way, as gives us breath:
Such a Truth, as ends all strife:
Such a Life, as killeth death.

Come, my Light, my Feast, my Strength: 5
Such a Light, as shows a feast:
Such a Feast, as mends in length:
Such a Strength, as makes his guest.

Come, my Joy, my Love, my Heart:
Such a Joy, as none can move: 10
Such a Love, as none can part:
Such a Heart, as joys in love.

The Big Picture

This is a petition of pure praise and joy. Usually Christians think of "call" as something initiated by God. Here, the opposite is true. This is a "call" to Jesus to come to the speaker in all of the ways described in the poem.

The Parts of the Picture

Stanza 1. Jesus is addressed in the manner in which he describes himself in John 14:6. Then (as in each stanza) each of the descriptive elements in the first line is given further comment.

Stanza 2. Here are more biblical allusions to Jesus as Light (John 8:12), Feast (probably John 6:53-59), and Strength (possibly John 6:57; Matthew 7:24-25, and/or I Peter 2:4-9). The "Feast" is the centerpiece of this stanza. It is not only a reference to Jesus as the Bread of Life but also to the Eucharist. It is referred to in three of the four lines of the stanza. Jesus as Light reveals the Feast; this Feast "mends" (or makes whole) "in length" or in its lengthening or extending of itself; and it "makes" Strength for the guest of Jesus or the one who partakes of the Feast or the Eucharist. F. E. Hutchinson describes the action here as "the divine light sets off the festival scene; it is a feast which improves as it goes on… and the Eucharistic feast is for 'the strengthening and refreshing of our souls.'"[49]

Stanza 3. Biblical allusions are here, also. Jesus is Joy which cannot be taken away (John 16:22). Jesus is the Father's expression of Love (John 3:16, among others) from which the speaker cannot be parted (John 10:28-30 and Romans 8:38-39). Jesus is also the speaker's Heart, his centerpiece and the wellspring that enables him to find joy in love. Throughout this stanza, there is an interweaving of Joy and Love as they are mentioned separately in lines 10 and 11 and brought together in line 12. And here, also, is an emphasis on the permanency of the relationship with Jesus that cannot be moved or parted (lines 10 and 11).

The Parts of the Picture Come Together

The poem is remarkable for its sustained focus on Jesus. Every word in this poem is directed to Jesus. He is called ("Come"); he is claimed ("my"); he is characterized (Way, Truth, Life, etc.); and he is praised ("gives us breath," "ends all strife," etc.).

There are at least two movements of thought. First, there is the movement within each stanza. The first line of each stanza, after calling for Jesus to come, characterizes Jesus with three nouns. This description is concentrated tightly with these three nouns that are personalized by the repetition of "my." Each element of this first line of concentrated description is then opened and extended in the next three lines. In the first stanza, for example, Way gives breath, Truth ends strife, and Life kills death. All of this movement from concentration to opening up is accomplished with a constant focus on Jesus.

The second movement of thought is from stanza to stanza. While the attention remains tightly focused on Jesus and the personalized claim on him is never relinquished throughout the poem, the emphasis on Jesus' nature is expanded with each stanza. In the first stanza, there is an emphasis on a central biblical image of Jesus as Way, Truth, and Life. In the second stanza, there are Eucharistic images of Light, Feast, and Strength. Finally, in the third stanza, experiential images of Joy, Love, and the Heart emerge and are given the quality of permanence ("none can move" and "none can part").

All of these movements and images are marvelously woven together in an invitation, a soft plea, a calling for Jesus to come. In one way, it is a Eucharistic prayer for the presence of Jesus. But in a larger way, it is a calling for the Word to become present at any place, at any time, and in a most personal manner, a manner that indeed changes things.

Reflections

1. What does this poem have to say about relationship with God?
2. What spiritual direction does it provide?
3. How do you respond to the characterizations of Jesus in this poem? Which ones are the most appealing to you?
4. This poem is a prayer "calling" Jesus to come. If you were praying such a prayer, how would you go about it? How many of the characteristics of Jesus mentioned in this poem would you use? What others would you add?

Scriptures for further reflection:

John 6:41-59
John 8:12; 12:35-36; and 12:46
John 14:5-6
John 15:1-11
Romans 8:38-39
Philippians 4:13

DEPENDING ON GOD

*H*erbert's dependence on God is reflected in varying degrees and in different perspectives in almost all of his poetry. The poems presented here are straightforward, definite, and unconditional declarations of this dependence. The first three of these poems deal with Herbert's vocational roles as priest and preacher. *The Priesthood* reflects Herbert's deep sense of unworthiness about being a priest and his even deeper sense of God's power to "vessels make of lowly matter." *Aaron* deals with the same problem in a similar way. Only in Christ is Herbert able to become an Aaron or true priest. In *The Windows* the focus is on the difficulty of the preacher proclaiming God's word. The solution again is found in God.

The other two poems under this heading focus on depending on God to overcome certain temptations. *Assurance* records the speaker's struggle with negative thoughts about his relationship with God. And *Conscience* deals with a similar struggle with "fears" brought about by the "peace prattler" and overcome by the blood and cross of Christ.

THE PRIESTHOOD

Blest Order, which in power dost so excel,
That with the one hand thou liftest to the sky,
And with the other throwest down to hell
In thy just censures; fain would I draw nigh,
Fain put thee on, exchanging my lay-sword   5
   For that of the holy Word.

But thou art fire, sacred and hallowed fire;
And I but earth and clay: should I presume
To wear thy habit, the severe attire
My slender compositions might consume.   10
I am both foul and brittle; much unfit
   To deal in holy Writ.

Yet have I often seen, by cunning hand
And force of fire, what curious things are made
Of wretched earth. Where once I scorned to stand,   15
That earth is fitted by the fire and trade
Of skillful artists, for the boards of those
   Who make the bravest shows.

But since those great ones, be they never so great,
Come from the earth, from whence those vessels come;   20
So that at once both feeder, dish, and meat
Have one beginning and one final sum:
I do not greatly wonder at the sight,
   If earth in earth delight.

But the holy men of God such vessels are,   25
As serve him up, who all the world commands:
When God vouchsafeth to become our fare,
Their hands convey him, who conveys their hands.
O what pure things, most pure must those things be,
   Who bring my God to me!   30

Wherefore I dare not, I, put forth my hand
To hold the Ark, although it seem to shake
Through the old sins and new doctrines of our land.
Only, since God doth often vessels make
Of lowly matter for high uses meet,   35
        I throw me at his feet.

There will I lie, until my Maker seek
For some mean stuff whereon to show his skill:
Then is my time. The distance of the meek
Doth flatter power. Lest good come short of ill   40
In praising might, the poor do by submission
        What pride by opposition.

The Big Picture

This poem deals with a particular vocational crisis Herbert faced in dealing with his call to the priesthood. The issue concerns the disparity between man and God: How could lowly man become a vessel used by God for his holy work? As the speaker tries to work through the difficulty of this calling, he is reminded of the purity of the "Blest Order" of the priesthood and of his own unworthiness. But he is also mindful that "God doth often vessels make/ Of lowly matter." His solution is to cast himself at the feet of God and to wait for God to "seek/ For some mean stuff whereon to show his skill."

The Parts of the Picture

Stanzas 1-2. The problem is presented. First, the "Blest Order" of priesthood is described with its power to lift or throw down (possible allusions to Matthew 16:19 and John 20:23). "Fain" or gladly would the speaker become a part of this Order, exchanging his "lay-sword" for the sword "of the holy Word" (see Ephesians 6:17). The contrast in stanza 2 brings into sharp focus the problem. The Order is "sacred and hallow'ed fire," and the speaker is "earth and clay." If he puts on the "attire" of the priesthood, it might "consume" the "slender compositions" of his body and mind. In short, the speaker is "much unfit" for the priesthood. Here is the introduction of the important images of fire (used in the Bible as an agent of the Holy, especially with regard to refining) and earth and clay (see Genesis 2:7 for the creation story's use of dust or earth and also see Jeremiah 18:6, Isaiah 64:8, and Romans 9:21 for imagery of man as clay and God as potter).

Stanzas 3-4. Having presented the problem of his unworthiness, the speaker now begins to work toward a solution. He begins with a secular analogy. He has often seen "curious things" made of "wretched earth" by "cunning hand/ And force of fire" (another use of the refining power of fire with another use in line 16). The earth on which he has "scorn'd to stand" has been "fitted" by "skillful artists" for use on "the boards" (or serving tables) of those distinguished by their bravery. With this illustration of how secular artists can transform "wretched earth" into dinnerware for the "bravest," the speaker has begun the process of his argument that there is hope for unfit "earth" such as he. In stanza 4, the argument is extended to the point that earth is associated with delight, a far cry from its previous association with being unfit (line 8). To demonstrate the goodness of earth, the speaker points out that, when "these great ones" (presumably a reference to those associated with "bravest shows" of line 18) use the dishware made from earth to serve the meat at meals, at that moment all of the elements—the "feeder, dish, and meat"—are united not only in that event but in their beginning as earth. Therefore, the speaker implies, there is hope for earth to be put to good use.

Stanza 5-6. But the problem is not yet resolved. The speaker returns to the "Blest Order" by considering another meal: the Eucharist when God mercifully condescends to "become our fare" or meal. Since the men of the priesthood convey God to His people in the Eucharist, pure must they be. Where does that leave the speaker? Stanza 6 gives the answer. He dares not reach out for "the Ark" or that which is Holy such as the Blest Order (see 2 Samuel 6:6-7 for the story of Uzzah who died as a result of reaching out for the Ark). He is not to do this even if the Ark needs to be steadied as a result of the "old sinnes and new doctrines of our land." Instead, the speaker will go a different route. He will throw himself alone at the feet of God since God seems to make use of "lowly matter for high uses."

Stanza 7. At the feet of God he will lie until his time comes. That time will be decided by God, a time when He decides to use some small or "mean stuff" to show His skills. In concluding, the speaker quotes a proverb in lines 39b and 40a, and then in the concluding two and one-half lines, he elaborates on it. F. E. Hutchinson's commentary on these concluding three and one-half lines is most helpful: "The modest by observing a respectful deference pay a better homage than the proud who seek to keep up their state by rival magnificence. Herbert may hope to commend himself for the priesthood by his humility."[50]

The Parts of the Picture Come Together

During part of his time at Cambridge, Herbert served as university orator. His expertise in rhetoric is apparent in this poem with its carefully constructed argument. The poem begins with the problem—the desire of the speaker to "put on" the priesthood and the vast gap between him (he is "both foul and brittle") and the "sacred and hallowed fire" of this Blest Order. Then with the "Yet" at the beginning of stanza 3, the poem takes a turn and heads toward resolving this problem. The argument begins in the secular realm. It concerns the transformation of "wretched earth" by skillful artists into "curious things" made for the serving "boards" of distinguished people, "those/Who make the bravest shows." When food is served on these "curious things" (presumably china), earth is the source of the people, the china dishes, and the meat being served. What is portrayed here is a lavish, delightful secular scene made possible by the transformation of earth into the elements of the scene. An important point has been established: the lowly (i.e., the earth) can be transformed into elements that make for delight.

The speaker now takes the principle established in this secular example and applies it to the priesthood. Just as earth is transformed into things of delight in the secular world, God transforms lowly humans for His work. In short, God enables priests to "serve him up" and "convey him" when He "vouchsafeth to become our fare" in the Eucharist. The key, then, to resolving the speaker's problem is in God's ability to transform—to purify humans for holy causes. Extending this truth to his own situation, the speaker decides on his plan. Her will not take the initiative and "reach" for the Blest Order. Instead, he will throw himself at the feet of God and wait for Him to make vessels "of lowly matter" (such as the speaker) for "high uses" (such as the priesthood).

The way to the priesthood is clear. It is in God's hands. The speaker will wait until God moves. The key for him is humility. The way to the priesthood is the way of "the poor," the way of submission. Ironically, the resolution to the problem is found in the problem itself—the wretched state of the speaker described in stanza 2. It is the speaker's humble recognition of his state that will provide the opportunity for God to move with His transforming power.

Reflections

1. What does this poem have to say about relationship with God?

2. What spiritual direction does it provide?

3 The poem is obviously about the speaker's call to the priesthood, but meditation on this poem can raise larger issues about God's use of humans for his works, whether inside or outside the priesthood. Is there a difference in what is required of humans in order for them to be used by God in the priesthood and in what is required of humans to be used by God in any other vocation? In short, is submission the key to our giving of ourselves to God to be used in any vocation?

4. Submission is the key to relationship with God. Do you agree? Why or why not?

5. What is the strongest force in your life that works against humility?

Scriptures for further reflection:

Psalm 25:9
Matthew 18:1-4
Matthew 20:20-28
Matthew 21:1-5
II Corinthians 4:7
II Corinthians 12:7-10
Philippians 2:8
James 4:6 and 10

AARON

Holiness on the head,
Light and perfections on the breast,
Harmonious bells below, raising the dead
To lead them unto life and rest:
Thus are true Aarons drest.   5

Profaneness in my head,
Defects and darkness in my breast,
A noise of passions ringing me for dead
Unto a place where is no rest:
Poor priest thus am I drest.   10

Only another head
I have, another heart and breast,
Another music, making live not dead,
Without whom I could have no rest:
In him I am well drest.   15

Christ is my only head,
My alone only heart and breast,
My only music, striking me even dead;
That to the old man I may rest,
And be in him new drest.   20

So holy in my head,
Perfect and light in my dear breast,
My doctrine tuned by Christ, (who is not dead,
But lives in me while I do rest)
Come people; Aaron's drest.   25

The Big Picture

This poem is about the difference Christ makes. To portray this difference, Herbert uses contrast, beginning with a description of the priest Aaron and the glorious elements of his dress and then moving to the defects of the speaker. This beginning contrast is followed by the description of the transformation of the speaker by the newness of life brought by Christ. Through Christ, the speaker has found righteousness that enables him to be like "Aaron drest."

The Parts of the Picture

Biblical Background. Aaron is the brother of Moses and Israel's first high priest. See Exodus 28 about Aaron's garments for consecration.

Structure. This is another of Herbert's pattern poems in which the structure of the poem conveys a part of its meaning. It is built on the number five. There are five stanzas, five lines in each stanza, five letters in Aaron, and the same five words appear as the ending words of the lines in each stanza. The outer pattern of the poem thereby stays the same (five stanzas, five lines in each stanza, etc.), but the inner content of the poem is transformed just as the speaker is by Christ.

Stanza 1. This presents the dress of "true Aarons." The "Holiness on the head" refers to the golden plate with the engraving "Holy to the Lord" that is fastened to the front of the turban worn by Aaron (see Exodus 28:36-38). The "Light and perfections on the breast" represent the Urim and Thummim on the breastplate over Aaron's heart (see Exodus 28:30). The "Harmonious bells below" are the bells of gold on the "skirts of the robe" of Aaron (see Exodus 28:33-34). The robe with the sound of its bells are associated with life since the sound of the bells must be heard when Aaron goes into and out of the place of the Lord (the Holy of Holies) or he will die (see Exodus 28:35). These bells, then, when worn by the priest are associated with the resurrection, power of raising "the dead/ To lead them unto life and rest" (lines 3-4).

Stanza 2. The poem moves from the dress of "true Aarons" to the actual dress of the speaker as a "poor priest." Contrast prevails. Rather than the holiness of the true priest, there is the "profaneness" of the speaker. Rather than "light and perfections," there are "defects and darkness" in his breast. And in place of the life giving bells, there is "the noise of passions ringing" death.

Stanzas 3-4. Here the speaker is transformed as he is dressed in "another head.... another heart and breast,/ Another music" in which he finds rest and is "well drest." This is new life in Christ with the dying to his old self (line 18, "striking me even dead") and the emerging of his new life in Christ (being "in him [Christ] new drest," (line 20).

Stanza 5. The speaker is now the true priest, now able to welcome people since it is Christ who lives in him while his old self of stanza 2 does "rest" (echoes of Galatians 2:20).

The Parts of the Picture Come Together

What difference does the living presence of Christ make? What does it mean to say along with the Apostle Paul, "I live, yet not I, but Christ liveth in me"? The speaker begins to deal with these questions with a portrait of Aaron, the archetypal priest of the Old Testament. The emphasis is on the externals of his dress—the head piece, the breastplate, the bells associated with life hanging from the clothing. This is a form of purity clearly prescribed in Exodus 28. It has the power of "raising the dead," leading them "unto life and rest."

But for the speaker, the externals are of no avail. Aaron's dress is not available to him. In contrast, the speaker is profane with defects and darkness and passions that provide no rest. Alone in this state, the speaker is bereft. But he is not alone—and on this the poem turns toward triumph. It is a triumph not achieved by the speaker himself and not found in his efforts, devices, or possessions. It is a victory not attained in the externals of dress. It is found only in another's head, heart, breast, and music. It is new life in Christ. And the new life comes from a death, a death of the old self, and from a new birth as the head, heart, breast, and music of Christ now clothe the speaker. Now alive in Christ, he is now ready to invite others into relationship with his closing "Come people: Aaron's drest."

The externals of the poem remain the same throughout (five stanzas, five lines in each stanza, five rhymes using the same words throughout), but the power of the poem is found in the complete transformation of the speaker. And the key is Christ. In Him is the dying of the self and the rising to newness of life in head and heart. In Him comes the opening of the self to others as the new self invites the people to "Come." Here is the difference Christ makes.

Reflections

1. What does the poem have to say about relationship with God?
2. What spiritual direction does it provide?
3. How would you describe the difference Christ has made in your life? Perhaps listing the differences in columns designated "Without Christ" and "With Christ" would be helpful. What differences have you not allowed Him to make?
4. Did the transformation brought by Christ come to you quickly or more gradually over a period of time or as a combination of both?
5. The speaker describes the difference made by Christ in his life within the vocational setting of his being a priest. What would be the setting of your description of the difference Christ has made in your life? Would it be a vocational setting, as in this poem, or would it be that of another dimension of your life, or both, or neither?

Scriptures for further reflection:

Mark 8:34-35
Romans 6:4
Galatians 2:20
Philippians 4:11-13
Colossians 2:13

THE WINDOWS

Lord, how can man preach thy eternal word?
        He is a brittle crazy glass:
Yet in thy temple thou dost him afford
           This glorious and transcendent place,
           To be a window, through thy grace.   5

But when thou dost anneal in glass thy story,
        Making thy life to shine within
The holy preacher's; then the light and glory
           More reverend grows, and more doth win:
           Which else shows waterish, bleak, and thin.   10

Doctrine and life, colors and light, in one
        When they combine and mingle, bring
A strong regard and awe: but speech alone
           Doth vanish like a flaring thing,
           And in the ear, not conscience ring.   15

The Big Picture

How can "brittle" man effectively preach God's word? The answer is not found in man's abilities, training, or education, although Herbert valued these. The answer is found in God and in His ability to reveal Himself through the preacher. In short, the poem celebrates God's power to transform the preacher and his deficiencies into a window of revelation of God's glory and light.

The Parts of the Picture

Structure. The first line poses a question that the rest of the poem answers. The first stanza presents the problem; the second stanza provides the answer; and the third draws the poem to a conclusion.

Stanza 1 states the issue: How can brittle, broken man preach God's eternal word?

The **second stanza** contains the answer. It is akin to the process of annealing a window (line 6). In this process the glass is heated and then cooled and thereby strengthened as the internal tensions causing its brittleness are removed. The colors painted on the glass become fixed in it. Through this process God places His "story" in the glass.

Stanza 3 concludes by giving a portrayal of the preacher's life with and without God's transforming work. The first two and one-half lines of the stanza present the preacher's life with God's work; the concluding two and one-half lines portray the preacher without God's transforming work.

The Parts of the Picture Come Together

Herbert was a preacher and thought deeply about his role. He deals with the subject in great detail in his classic prose work, A Priest to the Temple: The Country Parson, His Character and Rule of Holy Life. Briefly but intensely in this poem, Herbert focuses on the foundational aspect of the preacher's role—God alone enables the preacher to be a window to God. And fascinating is the way in which God performs His work.

The tension of the poem arises out of two seemingly opposed realities: man is "a brittle crazy [or cracked] glass," but God enables man, in his preaching, to be a window, a "glorious and transcendent place." The cracked glass is transformed by God, through His grace, into a window, something glorious and transcendent through which others are able to see God. How can this be?

A "window-making" process is the basic metaphor used to describe God's work. The annealing of a window produces strength and fixes colors in the window. It is a process that depends on heat and consequent cooling. By analogy, God writes His story in the brittle glass of the preacher through a process of applying heat and then cooling while fixing colors in the glass, thereby producing a window in which God's story is portrayed. The result is that God's life shines within the "holy Preacher's," giving him a winsome reverent "light and glory." Without this act of God's grace, the preacher's life and work would be "waterish, bleak, and thin."

In choosing this analogy, Herbert evokes thoughts of the biblical tradition of using an artisan to portray the manner of God's molding and making His people. For example, Jeremiah (18:3-4) speaks of God as a potter molding his people as clay. The annealing process with its essential element of using heat is also reminiscent of biblical images of the refining power of fire (see Numbers 31:21-23 and Isaiah 6:6-7). This use of heat to refine and mold the preacher has also been associated with the necessity of suffering in the molding of Christ-likeness in Christians, as Paul spoke of in Philippians 1:29 and Romans 8:17. All of this is God's work and only God's work.

Thus by God's grace the preacher's life is merged with the doctrine he preaches; the "talk" and "walk" of the preacher become one. As a result, "colors and light ... combine and mingle" producing "a strong regard and awe." This is an effect made possible because the preacher has become a window to God. But the preacher without God's transforming work (lines 13b-15) is mere talk or "speech alone," a flare vanishing quickly, devoid of good result, a "noisy gong and clanging cymbal" with no power to stir the reader's conscience.

Reflections

The poem focuses on the life of the preacher, but it obviously has application beyond the preacher. All of us as Christians share the need, with the preacher, to be windows to God by being God's witnesses. Perhaps the following questions will assist in your reflections about this matter of God's shaping our lives so that our light may shine for His glory:

1. What does the poem have to say about relationship with God?
2. What spiritual direction does it provide?
3. In what ways has God shaped your life so that you may be a "window" to Him? In what manner has this "shaping" taken place?
4. The poem speaks of the necessity of God's shaping His servant for His glory. As God's servant, do you also have a role in that process? How would you describe that role?
5. How do you resist God's molding and refining you?

Scriptures for further reflection:

Exodus 4:10-12
I Kings 3:5-9
Psalm 23:1
Jeremiah 1:6-8
Matthew 28:20
Acts 18:9-10
James 1:22-25

ASSURANCE

    O spiteful bitter thought!
Bitterly spiteful thought! Couldst thou invent
So high a torture? Is such poison bought?
Doubtless, but in the way of punishment.
        When wit contrives to meet with thee,   5
        No such rank poison can there be.

    Thou saidst but even now,
That all was not so fair, as I conceived,
Betwixt my God and me; that I allow
And coin large hopes, but that I was deceived: 10
        Either the league was broke, or near it;
        And, that I had great cause to fear it.

    And what to this? what more
Could poison, if it had a tongue, express?
What is thy aim? wouldst thou unlock the door   15
To cold despairs, and gnawing pensiveness?
        Wouldst thou raise devils? I see, I know,
        I writ thy purpose long ago.

    But I will to my Father,
Who heard thee say it. O most gracious Lord,   20
If all the hope and comfort that I gather,
Were from myself, I had not half a word,
        Not half a letter to oppose
        What is objected by my foes.

    But thou art my desert: 25
And in this league, which now my foes invade,
Thou art not only to perform thy part,
But also mine; as when the league was made
        Thou didst at once thy self indite,
        And hold my hand, while I did write.   30

Wherefore if thou canst fail,
Then can thy truth and I: but while rocks stand,
And rivers stir, thou canst not shrink or quail:
Yea, when both rocks and all things shall disband,
    Then shalt thou be my rock and tower,   35
    And make their ruin praise thy power.

Now foolish thought go on,
Spin out thy thread, and make thereof a coat
To hide thy shame: for thou hast cast a bone
Which bounds on thee, and will not down thy throat: 40
    What for itself love once began,
    Now love and truth will end in man.

The Big Picture

How is doubt to be handled? Here Herbert handles it aggressively by taking the initiative to find the assurance of comfort and hope in the Father. The speaker works out his struggle with a dramatic response to a threatening thought of doubt (lines 1-18), with a petition/praise to the Father (lines 19-36), and finally with an exclamation of victory over that doubt (lines 37-42).

The Parts of the Picture

Stanzas 1-3. In these stanzas, the speaker responds to a "spiteful bitter thought." The two exclamations that open the poem suddenly and dramatically present the heightened intensity of the situation. The two questions that follow ask for, with continued intensity, the source of this thought. Was its "torture" invented, its "poison bought"? Doubtless, the thought has been "invented" or "bought," but only "in the way of punishment." When "wit" (or keen, quick intelligence) "contrives" with such a "spiteful bitter thought," the poison that results is unmatched by any other poison. And what is the content of the thought? The second stanza provides the answer. The thought is aimed at destroying the speaker's relationship with God. The speaker believes this relationship to be "fair" (or just and appropriate) and with "large hopes." The thought of doubt calls all this into question, declaring that the speaker has been deceived, that the "league" (or the relationship between speaker and God) is "broke, or near it" and that there is "great cause to fear it." The third stanza concludes this opening address to the "spiteful bitter thought" by questioning the "aim" of this thought. Is not the "aim" to "unlock the door/ To cold despairs, and gnawing pensiveness," and "raise devils"? The speaker knows the purpose of this thought since he has written its "purpose long ago" (perhaps a reference to the speaker's previous dealings with previous bitter thoughts).

Stanzas 4-6. The speaker, having dealt with the content and purpose of doubt, now turns toward assurance. That is to be found in "my Father," "the most gracious Lord" who has heard the attack by the thought of doubt. The first expression to the Father is a confession of dependence. On his own, the speaker has no hope of "hope and comfort," "not half a word, / Not half a letter to oppose" his foes. But, as the first line of stanza 5 points out, the speaker knows that in God is he found deserving. The "foes" have now invaded "this league" between the speaker and God, but God will perform both his and the speaker's "part" just as He did when "the league was made." Perhaps this "league" refers to the new covenant made possible by the crucifixion. At that time, God did write ("indite") for himself and held the speaker's hand as he wrote or signed on to the league. Stanza 6 draws a conclusion, as indicated by "Wherefore." It is a conclusion of confidence expressed in God's power to prevail over all and remain "when all things disband." The imagery here of God as refuge is possibly rooted in passages such as Psalm 18:1-3; 31:3-5; and 61:1-3.

Stanza 7. The speaker now returns to addressing the "thought." This thought is now "foolish" (after being addressed as "spiteful bitter" in the opening lines). Images associated with it are ones of defeat. The speaker directs the thought to spin "his thread" to "make thereof a coat/*To hide thy shame* [emphasis added]." The bone of contention cast by the thought has boomeranged ("bounds on thee") and is now caught in its throat, choking it. The concluding couplet ends triumphantly on a note of love: what love began for itself (perhaps God's power of love in the beginning) is now completed by "love and truth" (or perhaps "assurance") in man.

The Parts of the Picture Come Together

The poem begins with feelings, the raw feelings of the speaker responding to a "thought" that has come to him. The feelings are expressed in angry exclamations accompanied by piercing rhetorical questions. The point is abundantly clear: the "thought" is spiteful, bitter, torturous, poisonous, punishing. To say that the impact of the thought on the speaker is dramatic is an understatement.

Having dramatized the emotional impact of the thought, the speaker then tries to understand by dealing with the content of the thought. This thought questions and undermines the speaker's relationship with God by claiming that the speaker has been deceived and has "great cause to fear" the brokenness of the relationship. And what is the purpose behind all this? Is it not to loose "cold despairs" and "gnawing pensiveness," and "raise devils"?

This initial thrust of the poem has enabled the speaker to express his distress and define the problem. It is a problem of ultimate significance in that it threatens the speaker's relationship with God. It is a problem that evokes a response of highly charged emotions. It is problem designed to punish, to bring about the devilish chaos of despair. Beyond this outburst of feelings, how is the speaker to respond? The "thought" is victorious if the speaker's only response is emotional upheaval.

The poem takes a turn as the speaker turns to the Father. The tone changes. Emotions remain, but gone is the anger, the resentment, the nearness of despair. What occurs is the beginning of assurance. It begins with a release, a submission, an expression of dependence on the Father. It continues with an acknowledgment of presence of this dependence since the beginning of the "league" between the speaker and the Father. And assurance comes to a climax as the speaker proclaims the power and permanence of the Father and of their relationship.

In the comfort and hope found in the Father, the speaker pronounces the defeat of the "foolish thought." The thought has been rendered powerless. Instead of spinning bitter, spiteful poisons, it now spins a coat to hide its shame. Rather than threatening despair with its utterances, it is silenced as it chokes on the bone of contention that has rebounded and is caught in the throat of the thought. The love and truth that were denied by the thought are triumphant in man. Such assurance!!

The poem has moved from the bitterness of raw emotional response, to finding assurance in the Father, and finally to the victory over the thought that denied truth and love. In short, doubt is defeated by acknowledging its destructive impact, by coming to an understanding of its purpose, by submitting to the Father and finding the security of His assurance, and finally by pronouncing the failure of the thought and the triumph of love and truth.

Reflections

1. What does this poem have to say about relationship with God?
2. What spiritual direction does it provide?
3. What are the different kinds of doubt that you have encountered? Which kind(s) is (are) the most difficult to deal with?
4. What benefits can be derived from doubt?
5. How do you respond to doubt? Does it depend on the circumstances and the nature of the doubt?
6. What kind of assurance has come to you from your experiences with doubt? In what ways has it come? Has assurance always resolved your doubt? What do you do when it does not?

Scriptures for further reflection:

Psalm 18:1-2
Psalm 23
Psalm 31:3-5
Psalm 61:1-3
Psalm 73:23-28
Habakkuk 3:17-19

CONSCIENCE

Peace prattler, do not lour:
Not a fair look, but thou dost call it foul:
Not a sweet dish, but thou dost call it sour:
Music to thee doth howl.
By listening to thy chatting fears   5
I have both lost mine eyes and ears.

Prattler, no more, I say:
My thoughts must work, but like a noiseless sphere;
Harmonious peace must rock them all the day:
No room for prattlers there.   10
If thou persist, I will tell thee,
That I have physic to expel thee.

And the receipt shall be
My Saviour's blood: whenever at his board
I do but taste it, straight it cleanseth me,   15
And leaves thee not a word;
No, not a tooth or nail to scratch,
And at my actions carp, or catch.

Yet if thou talkest still,
Besides my physic, know there's some for thee: 20
Some wood and nails to make a staff or bill
For those that trouble me:
The bloody cross of my dear Lord
Is both my physic and my sword.

The Big Picture

A good place to begin is the title. What kind of conscience is the subject of the poem? John Tobin points out that conscience here is not to be understood as "the voice of God or of the Holy Spirit, but as a troubling agent reminding the speaker of his failings..."[52] In dealing with this subject, Herbert personifies conscience, using a monologue directed to it and characterizing it as a "peace prattler" (a disturber of the peace). After painting out the negative effects of this prattler, the speaker turns to the medicine that cleanses him: the "bloody cross of my dear Lord" which provides him both medicine (in the Eucharist) for cleansing and a sword to attack. In short, the poem is both a commentary on the negative effects of this kind of conscience and the triumphant power of the cross as an antidote to these effects.

The Parts of the Picture

Stanza 1. Here is the problem. The disturber of the peace is confronted with an instruction not to frown or scowl. What follows is a listing of the negative effects of this conscience: fair looks are made foul; sweet dishes become sour; music howls; and the "chatting fears" of conscience harm the speaker's "eyes and ears."

Stanza 2. A twofold response to the "prattler" begins. First, the speaker's thoughts are to work like a "noiseless sphere," dominated by "harmonious peace." Secondly, if the "prattler" remains, the speaker will expel him with medicine.

Stanza 3. The "receipt" nature or formula of the "physic" or medicine is revealed. It is his "Savior's blood" tasted in the Eucharist at "his board" (or Communion table) which cleanses as the "prattler" is disarmed with nothing left over by which he can cast his negative "word."

Stanza 4. There is one more device to be used against this conscience: the wood and nails of the cross which can be made into a staff or "a bill" (a spear). The two functions of the cross are summarized in the poem's final lines.

The Parts of the Picture Come Together

The poem moves through various stages with increasing intensity as the speaker acknowledges and confronts his conscience. First, the speaker describes the power of this "disturber of the peace." Good things such as fair looks, sweet dishes, and music are given a negative cast by this conscience. It operates by depriving the speaker of his senses by which he can find direction. Indeed, this is a formidable opponent. But there is another dimension of the problem. The speaker opens himself to the "chatting fears" spoken by the conscience and thereby becomes involved himself in the making of his problem.

Then the poem turns. As he continues to address his conscience, the speaker makes a vow. This is the first step in his recovery—by turning from passive listening to becoming the active participant that confronts negativity. He formulates a plan. Peace is the goal, and the speaker has the medicine that will be the means of achieving that goal. But rather than taking the road of self-sufficiency, the speaker looks to the Savior's blood, tasted in the Eucharist, to cleanse him of conscience's negative powers. And there is more. If the conscience persists, the speaker will use "wood and nails" as a staff or sword. As David in Psalm 23 takes comfort in the rod and staff of the Lord, so, too, the speaker here sees the cross as his staff with which to do battle with this "prattler."

It is a poem that begins with the power of negativity and ends with the defeat of that power. It is a poem in which the speaker makes a vow, formulates a plan, and then reaches outside himself to the resources of his Savior for cleansing of the power of his opponent. It is a poem in which the transforming power of Christ's "bloody cross" is made clear. It is a poem in which human resolve and the resources made available by Christ come together as God intended—to defeat a force that negates goodness and drains life.

Reflections

1. What does the poem have to say about relationship with God?
2. What spiritual direction does it offer?
3. How do you react to negativity that transforms goodness into life-draining forces?
4. As the speaker reaches beyond himself to the life cleansing powers of Christ, he resists the temptation to resort to self-sufficiency in dealing with his problem. How do you deal with this temptation in this kind of situation?

Scriptures for further reflection:

John 6:52-59
Romans 3:23-25
Hebrews 9:11-14
Revelation 5:9-10

GRIEF

*H*erbert often used his poetry to work through the grief of difficult times (for example, see *The Cross*, *Affliction (I)*, *The Search*, *Denial*, and *Employment*). In the two poems under this heading, Herbert focuses on one thing: God is at work in the grief.

JOSEPH'S COAT

Wounded I sing, tormented I indite,
Thrown down I fall into a bed, and rest:
Sorrow hath changed its note: such is his will,
Who changeth all things, as him pleaseth best.
    For well he knows, if but one grief and smart   5
Among my many had his full career,
Sure it would carry with it even my heart,
And both would run until they found a bier
    To fetch the body; both being due to grief.
But he hath spoiled the race; and given to anguish   10
One of Joy's coats, ticing it with relief
To linger in me, and together languish.
    I live to show his power, who once did bring
    My joys to weep, and now my griefs to sing.

The Big Picture

How do you process your sorrow? Or, perhaps more importantly, do you see God at work in your sorrow? This poem reveals a way of processing grief in which God is very much at work. In the midst of the speaker's being wounded, tormented, and thrown down, he is able to sing, write, and rest because God has changed sorrow's note and "spoiled the race" for grief.

The Parts of the Picture

The Title. The title alludes to the story of Joseph in which Jacob gives his favorite son Joseph a coat of many colors, thereby provoking Joseph's jealous brothers to take harmful action against him. See Genesis 37.

Lines 1-4. The first two lines describe the speaker's response to grief, and lines 3 and 4 give the reason for the action described in the initial two lines. Because the speaker sings when wounded, writes when tormented, and rests when thrown down, sorrow's note is changed. All this is God's will.

Lines 5-9. Joseph Summers points out that this is "a strange sonnet with an un-rhymed first line." It is also "strange" in that usually there is a division of thought concluding with line 8, but here the division comes after line 9. These five lines give an illustration of what it would have been like if God had not changed sorrow's note. If "one grief and smart" would have had its way completely (or "had his full career"), it would have swept away the speaker's heart till both the grief and his heart found a "bier" on which to carry his corpse - all this "due to grief." F. E. Hutchinson's comment on pronouns and their antecedents is helpful: "In line 8 both means one grief and smart (a single conception, followed by singular pronouns, his, it) and my heart, but in line 9 both appears to be my heart and the body."

Lines 10-14. But God "hath spoiled the race" that is described in lines 5 through 9. He has done so by giving to anguish "One of Joy's coats," enticing ("ticing") anguish to "linger" in the speaker while there "together" the Joy and the anguish "languish" or diminish as they nullify each other. This description of God's working to "spoil the race" of grief and anguish sets up the concluding couplet which is a tribute to God's power to both bring joy to weep and grief to sing.

The Parts of the Picture Come Together

God (the "he" and "his" and "him" of lines 3, 4, 5, 10, and 13) is the driving force of this poem. It is God who changed sorrow's note (line 3a) as He changes all things as He pleases (lines 3b-4). It is God who knows what would have happened to the speaker if He had not "spoiled the race" (lines 5-10a). It is God who gave anguish "one of Joy's coats" (lines 10b-11a). And in the climactic conclusion, it is God for whom the speaker lives his life, showing God's power to bring Joy to weep and grief to sing.

But the poem is not merely general praise of God. It is, rather, a song of thanksgiving for God's power to move in a certain way in the midst of sorrow. The title of the poem alludes to the nature of that movement. Jacob gave the coat to Joseph in joy. The joy soon turned to sorrow as Joseph's brothers, out of jealously, banished him, resulting in his being imprisoned in Egypt. But out of that anguish, God raises Joseph to a position of immense power, second only to the Pharaoh of Egypt. This movement—from joy to sorrow to singing—is God's movement of power. As Joseph told his brothers as he saves them from their plight, "you meant evil against me; but God meant it unto good." (Genesis 50:20) It is this power for which the speaker lives.

And so the parts of the poem come together as praise for God's power. From the opening description of how God enables the speaker to respond to sorrow (lines 1-4), through the illustration of God's spoiling the race of grief toward destruction (lines 5-12), and finally to the climactic couplet in which the speaker praises God's power to move from the heights of joy to the weeping of grief and back to the joy of singing—in all of this movement, it is the speaker recognizing, describing, exalting, and finding his reason for existing in the power of God to spoil the race of grief and thereby deliver the speaker from its grasp.

Reflections

1. What does this poem have to say about relationship with God?
2. What spiritual direction does it provide?
3. How do you process your sorrow? Perhaps it depends on the nature of the circumstances. Or perhaps you have a certain way of dealing with sorrow no matter the circumstances. Is this poem helpful in developing an approach to dealing with sorrow?
4. Have you experienced God at work in the midst of your sorrow? If so, how would you describe it? Perhaps you have experienced the fact that often the workings of God are not realized until the grief or sorrow begins to diminish and some perspective returns. In short, as indicated in this poem and in the story of Joseph's coat, discovering the workings of God in the midst of sorrow is often a matter of looking backwards at the completed events. Has this been your experience?

Scriptures for further reflection:

Deuteronomy 31:8
Psalm 23
Psalm 46:1
Psalm 121
Matthew 5:4
Romans 8:37-39
II Corinthians 1:3-4

AFFLICTION (III)

My heart did heave, and there came forth, O God!
By that I knew that thou wast in the grief,
To guide and govern it to my relief,
  Making a scepter of the rod:
   Hadst thou not had thy part,   5
Sure the unruly sigh had broke my heart.

But since thy breath gave me both life and shape,
Thou knowest my tallies; and when there's assigned
So much breath to a sigh, what's then behind?
  Or if some years with it escape,   10
   The sigh then only is
A gale to bring me sooner to my bliss.

Thy life on earth was grief, and thou art still
Constant unto it, making it to be
A point of honor, now to grieve in me,   15
  And in thy members suffer ill.
   They who lament one cross,
Thou dying daily, praise thee to thy loss.

The Big Picture

Life is full of losses. Whether caused by death, divorce, unemployment, illness, aging, moving, or otherwise, losses come—and grief is not far behind. This poem is about grief. It is also about God. It is a poem about the grief of the speaker (cause of grief unknown) and God's knowledge of and presence in this grief. It is a poem that does not comment on whether God causes the grief, but it does make clear that God is at work for good in the grief. It is, therefore, a poem of thanksgiving and concludes with muted praise, but the praise is stated in an unusual fashion as it is combined with a convicting thought about our insensitivity to God's loss in grief.

The Parts of the Picture

Stanza 1 states the speaker's realization of God's presence and redeeming work in his grief. In uttering "Oh, God," the poet realizes God's presence, "guiding and governing" his relief. In short, God has transformed the rod of grief (a striking image of the power of grief) into a scepter, a staff held by rulers to signify their authority. Without this work of God, the speaker's heart would have broken.

Stanza 2 is an aside on the importance of a "sigh" such as the one mentioned in the first stanza. This may seem odd to the modern reader, but it must be understood within the context of the thought of Herbert's time. In that time a sigh was thought to lessen one's strength and shorten one's life. As indicated in line 7 by the reference to God's giving the speaker his breath, this concept comes, at least in part, from the biblical notion of God's breathing life into man in the Genesis 2 creation story. Since it was thought that man was given only so much breath, a sigh would obviously lessen the amount of life left in him. Hence, there is the statement in line 8 that God knows the speaker's "tallies" or the account of what life he has left after his sigh. After the speaker considers how much time is left for him, he concludes, in lines 10-12, that if the sigh has taken years of life from him, it has merely brought him closer to his heavenly bliss. Why would the speaker go into this aside which seems to lead us away from his grief? First, it does not lead away from his grief; it merely deals with it in a more indirect fashion than in the first stanza. Secondly, this notion of a sigh's lessening strength and reducing life was a common poetic device of the day (used, for example, by John Donne in *A Valediction: of Weeping*). Thirdly, the speaker uses the notion to illustrate what his grief (accompanied by a sigh) has cost him. It would be the same as our indicating the agony of our grief by saying "it has taken years off my life." Simply put, to indicate the seriousness of the effect of his grief, the speaker has used this common poetic device. But quickly the poem turns in line 10 from what has been taken from the speaker to the positive view that, even if he has lost years off his life, the speaker has been brought sooner to his heavenly bliss. This movement from negative to positive in this stanza is consistent with the movement of the poem overall as the speaker throughout faces the cost of grief but always remains with the underlying premise that God is at work for good in that same grief.

Stanza 3 returns to focusing more directly on God at work. God's involvement is extended beyond the grief of the speaker. God's acquaintance with grief is twofold: first, His life on earth in Jesus was full of grief; and, secondly, He is "still constant into it" by "suffering ill" in the grief of the speaker and of others of His "members." Praise is the subject of the final two lines, but the praise is insufficient. The syntax of these two lines makes for a difficult reading. F. E. Hutchinson is most helpful (as usual) with his paraphrase of these lines in his commentary: "They who praise thee only for thy death on the cross, praise thee below thy deserts, for, by sharing in the grief and suffering of all thy members (lines 2, 16), thou diest daily."[56]

The Parts of the Picture Come Together

Where do we begin when we talk about grief? The speaker has started at one of the best places—with the experience of the one doing the grieving, with the grief of the speaker himself. But subtly and surely the poem moves from a focus on the poet's grief to a focus on God. To be sure, God is present throughout the poem, but while the first two stanzas speak of God, the primary focus is on the speaker. Note in the first stanza the references to "My heart," "I knew," "my relief," and "my heart." In stanza 2, there is "gave me," "my tallies," "bring me," and "my bliss." In the third stanza, however, while the speaker remains (but with only one explicit reference to him, in line 15), the emphasis is shifted to God as shown in the references to "Thy life," "thou art," "Thou dying," and "praise thee to thy loss." This movement in focus from the grief experienced by the speaker to the grief experienced by God represents the speaker's desire to move the reader from man to God. There is good reason for this because it is in God's continuing sacrifice of being constantly present to His people that their grief is "guided and governed" to relief. The speaker would have us to know that although our experience with grief always starts with our own loss and accompanying pain, the dealing with it moves toward God. The road through grief, in effect, runs through God.

Reflections

1. What does the poem have to say about relationship with God?
2. What spiritual direction does it provide?
3. How do you respond to grief? To your grief? To the grief of others? How does your response depend upon the circumstances? As the grief experience works itself out over time, is there a change or development in your focus and feelings?
4. How do you respond to God in your grief? With anger? Disbelief? Despair? Praise? A combination of these? Or otherwise? As the grief experience works itself out over time, is there a change or development in your feelings about God?
5. Of what value is the poem's perspective that God is with you in your grief, "guiding and governing it to your relief"? Of what value is its perspective that God "dies daily" through His presence with His people in their grief?

Scriptures for further reflection:

Isaiah 53
Mark 14:32-42
Mark 15
Hebrews 5:7

PRAYER

*P*rayer (I) is perhaps the most unusual of Herbert's poems. It defines prayer by bringing together a series of images. *The Storm* concerns one type of prayer: a persistent, aggressive kind. *The Method* deals with the correct method of prayer. The two poems concerning two of the fixed hours of prayers, *Matins* and *Evensong*, contain praise offered at the beginning and ending of the day, respectively.

PRAYER (I)

Prayer the Church's banquet, Angels' age,
     God's breath in man returning to his birth,
     The soul in paraphrase, heart in pilgrimage,
The Christian plummet sounding heaven and earth;
Engine against the Almighty, sinners' tower,   5
     Reversed thunder, Christ-side-piercing spear,
     The six-day's world transposing in an hour,
A kind of tune, which all things hear and fear;
Softness, and peace, and joy, and love, and bliss,
     Exalted Manna, gladness of the best,   10
     Heaven in ordinary, man well drest,
The milky way, the bird of Paradise,
     Church-bells beyond the stars heard, the soul's blood,
     The land of spices; something understood.

The Big Picture

This poem provides an unusual reading experience. As one scholar has pointed out, "the poem resists conventional definition" and "upsets any conventional expectations of how it might proceed." It challenges the reader's imagination in a manner unlike any of Herbert's other poems. For example, it is without a verb. Furthermore, it is in sonnet form but develops mostly without apparent regard for the conventional division of thought in a sonnet.

The comments of two scholars are helpful in coming to an understanding of the overall structure of the poem. First, Harold Bloom speaks of the images and metaphors used to describe prayer in the poem: "This astonishing sonnet deploys some two dozen superb tropes, all images of prayer…Prayer ingeniously becomes a sequence of metaphors, several of them gustatory: banquet, manna, well dressed, the land of spices." [58] And Joseph Summers has called the poem "an achievement in suggestion." [59] It "suggests" through a series of descriptions or images. Its suggestions are always about the nature of prayer.

The Parts of the Picture

The divisions of thought in the poem fall along the punctuation marks, primarily the commas found throughout. There are also semicolons at the end of lines 4 and 8 and in the middle of line 14 with a concluding period. This discussion of the parts of this poem will follow the order of these divisions. It will focus on the description of prayer within each division by discussing some possible meanings of each such description. As you consider each description, perhaps you can think of meanings in addition to those listed below.

Line 1a, "the Church's banquet"

Here is the first of several biblical allusions. Banquets are plentiful in the Bible. For example, the eschatological banquets of Isaiah 25:6 and Revelation 19:9, 17-18 celebrate God's final victory. There are the numerous occasions in which Jesus used a banquet setting for fellowship and teaching (for example, Luke 14:1-24 and the Last Supper).

A banquet is a unifying event, a time for people to come together for fellowship, nourishment, encouragement, and joy, as they did in the love feasts of the early church. Therefore, in describing prayer as "the Church's banquet," Herbert is suggesting that prayer is a unifying event, the church's opportunity for spiritual nourishment, for fellowship with God and (in public prayer) with each other, for joy, and for learning (considering Jesus used banquets for teaching).

For Herbert there is also the close association of banquet and the Eucharist, as indicated by his poem *The Banquet*.

Line 1b, "angel's age,"

F. E. Hutchinson says that "prayer acquaints man with the blessed timeless existence of the angels."[60] E. B. Greenwood, in a definitive article on this poem, points out that prayer is as old as the angels who were created to praise God.[61] See also Luke 20:36.

Line 2, "God's breath in man returning to his birth,"

The biblical allusion is to Genesis 2:7. Here there is an indication of prayer as a two way movement[62] since man and God reconnect. First, there is God's gift of breath at man's birth. Then man returns to God through prayer with the breath given by God. The union is full circle. Prayer is a rebirth of God and man's original connection.

Line 3a, "The soul in paraphrase,"

Hutchinson is again helpful here: "a paraphrase," he says, "... clarifies by expansion; in prayer the soul opens out and more fully discovers itself."[63] The myriad of ways in which the soul may "open out" are the ways of prayer itself, such as thanksgiving, praise, confession, and petition.

Line 3b, "heart in pilgrimage,"

The difference in "soul" in the previous phrase (line 3a) and "heart" in this phrase is probably minimal, if any. They both likely refer to that entity (inherently indefinable) which controls a person's affections and emotions. In the previous phrase (line 3a), prayer involves the "soul" expanding. In this phrase, prayer is the "heart in pilgrimage." Here is the journey motif, a strong biblical motif. Prayer concerns pilgrimage, its length, destination, duration, route, necessary tasks, joys, and hardships. Herbert's use of pilgrimage as a metaphor for the journey of life is made clear in his poem entitled *The Pilgrimage*. Hence, Herbert's use of pilgrimage in this poem about prayer brings the two ideas together in a way that emphasizes prayer as the heart's companion in life's pilgrimage.

Line 4, "The Christian plummet sounding heaven and earth;"

The phrase "plummet sounding" involves measuring the height and depth of something with a line attached to a piece of metal.[64] By way of comparison, prayer is the Christian taking a "sounding" of "heaven and earth." This may involve all kinds of plummeting—describing, evaluating, questioning, coming to an understanding, analyzing, experiencing mystery, discovering new knowledge. All or some of this plummeting of heaven and earth can be part of the experience of prayer.

Line 5a, "Engine against th' Almighty,"

Notice the change in tone in lines 5 and 6 as prayer is associated with strong, forceful images. Surprisingly, here in line 5a, prayer is described as something "against" God, perhaps expressing the kind of prayer found in laments and other prayers with protest of God's ways (see Job's laments and Jesus' cry in the Garden of Gethsemane to "take this cup from me"). John Tobin describes this phrase as "prayer as condoned aggression."[65] For biblical examples of prayer having the nature of importunity, see the following as examples: the prayer of Abraham in Genesis 18:22-33; the prayer of Moses in Numbers 11:10-15; Jeremiah in his "confessions" (Jeremiah 11:18-20; 12:1-6; 15:10-21; 17:14-18; 18:18-23; and 20:7-18); the psalmist in Psalms 6, 13, 25:1-7, and 51, to name a few; and Jesus in his teachings in Luke 11:5-8 and Luke 18-1-8.

Line 5b, "sinners' tower,"

One scholar describes this as "a benign inversion of the tower of Babel."[66] The Babel story itself (found in Genesis 11:1-9) is a tragic story of the sinfulness of men who built a tower into the heavens "to make a name for themselves." The benign inversion of that story in this poem comes as Herbert paradoxically inverts the meaning of the sinful tower imagery into a positive image portraying prayer as sinners' legitimate way of reaching for the heavens.

Line 6a, "Reversed thunder,"

Here is another inversion. Thunder comes down to earth, but here thunder is reversed or arises from below, presumably from the earth, as prayer. This opens several possibilities to consider:

1. Prayer is mankind's thunder, man's way of expressing all that is within, perhaps

142

akin to the "Engine against th' Almighty" in line 5a.

2. Prayer, through confession and petition and otherwise, is a way of reversing God's thunder or judgment. See Abraham's prayer in Genesis 18: 22-33.
3. Prayer is heard clearly and attracts attention, just as thunder is and does.
4. Prayer's power, like thunder's, comes from its being heard and not seen.
5. Just as thunder is jolting as it comes down from heaven, the power of prayer is jolting as it arises from below into the heavens.

Line 6b, "Christ-side-piercing spear,"

See John 19:34 for the image of the soldier piercing Jesus' side and the resulting flow of blood and water. In the flowing of the blood and water, God and man are united. In prayer, union (albeit a different kind) also occurs. With the flowing of the blood, the Eucharistic element is here also and, like prayer, signifies another union of God and man. In what ways are this spear and prayer similar? Do not each of them open God to man? Is it not the flowing of Jesus' blood that makes prayer possible?

Line 7, "The six-days world transposing in an hour,"

With the "transposing" of this line and the "kind of tune" in next line, the poet introduces musical imagery. The biblical allusion is to the creation story of Genesis 1. Coupled with line 2 of the poem, this is the second image from the creation story.

How does prayer, in an hour, transpose or transform, God's created world? Is this a comment on the creative (or re-creative) power of prayer? In prayer, are we able to see the world anew and see it as "very good" as God did? In effect, is the transposing power of prayer something that changes our view of the world, enabling us to see it as God did? Or is this a comment on prayer's ability, even in an hour, to reunite creation (including the creature who is praying) and Creator as they were at the end of the six days of Creation? Perhaps the power of one hour of prayer is to move God to renew, alter, affect, or otherwise transpose God's creation in a manner similar to that which occurred in the six days of Creation. In effect, the power of prayer triggers God's creative power.

Line 8a, "A kind of tune,"

Prayer is a melody, a sound arranged in a succession of notes, pleasing because of its arrangement and the emotions expressed.

Line 8b, "which all things hear and fear;"

Prayer is not only a "kind of tune," in and of itself, as stated in line 8a, it is also a specific kind of tune "which all things hear and fear." There are at least two interpretations to consider here. First, this is a comment on the power of mankind's prayer to God. Prayer is like a tune that is so powerful it can be heard and thereby feared by all things.

In short, the power of mankind's prayer is similar to a tune that is so powerful that it is heard and feared by all things. An alternative interpretation, or perhaps a complementary one with a different focus, is to see prayer as a kind of tune that is heard and feared by all things. Interpreted in this way, prayer is something coming from God to mankind and, because God is its source, it is heard and feared, or held in awe and reverence, by all of God's creation.

Line 9, "Softness, and peace, and joy, and love, and bliss,"

Prayer is each of these; and prayer is all of these.

Line 10a, "Exalted manna,"

Here is a return to the food imagery of "the Church's banquet" in line 1a. The biblical allusion is to God's providing daily manna to His people in the wilderness, as described in Exodus 16:15-16. Prayer is portrayed as a spiritual feeding, a gift from God, a union with God, a feeding exalted above that daily feeding in the wilderness in the Old Testament. This is another description with Eucharistic overtones, with "Exalted" manna being the "Bread of Heaven" of the Eucharist. E.B. Greenwood suggests that this is another example of prayer involving a two-way movement between man and God since the manna comes from heaven for mankind's feeding, and prayer is people returning this feeding to God as they exalt to God their petitions, confessions, praises, and other elements of prayer.

Line 10b, "gladness of the best,"

Three elements—prayer, gladness, and "the best"—are intermingled here. There are several possibilities of meaning, including the following: (1) Prayer is gladness resulting from "the best" kind of experience, prayer itself. (2) Prayer in itself is the best kind of gladness. (3) Prayer is gladness of people at their best in prayer.[67]

Line 11, "Heaven in ordinary, man well drest,"

The comma in this line, as elsewhere, marks a division of thought, but since there is a balance and contrast in this line that unites it, the line will be considered in its entirety while noting the division therein. "Heaven in ordinary" portrays prayer as bringing heaven into the ordinariness of life. Here is another incident of God coming to man in prayer (as in the Eucharistic images of the banquet in line 1 and the blood in line 6 and the bread in line 10; possibly in the creative power of line 7 and in the tune of line 8; and in the conditions described in line 9).

The other phrase, "man well drest," is a contrast to the movement of God to man in "Heaven in ordinary." Here the movement is man toward God. Here prayer is man's best dress with which to approach God. Prayer, in short, is the best way for man to approach God. But these two phrases in this line are not only in contrast, they complement one another as, together, they give us another image of the union of man and God in prayer. Hence, the line is both balanced and united, even with its contrasting elements.

Line 12a, "The milky way,"

Images of darkness and light come together here. Prayer as the milky way is the way to heaven. Prayer, in fact, lights up the heavens. Without it, there would be no light, no beauty, only darkness. Without it, there would be no way.

Line 12b, "bird of Paradise,"

The "bird of Paradise" is a peacock-like creature thought to live continually in the air. Prayer, then, is associated with the life of this kind of bird.

Line 13a, "Church-bells beyond the stars heard,"

Here again is the two-way nature of prayer. When we pray, we hear the music of heaven. On the other hand, when we pray, our prayer goes beyond the stars.

Line 13b, "the soul's blood."

Biblically, blood is essential to life and to sacrifice. It is the shedding of blood that is the center of Old Testament sacrifices and, of course, of Jesus' sacrifice for us. Medically, blood is essential to the life of the body. Spiritually, prayer is the "soul's blood," essential to the life of the soul. The reference to blood also ties in with the Eucharist.

Line 14a, "The land of spices;"

This term is associated with[68] the land of riches sought by explorers; with the land "flowing with milk and honey" that is the Promised Land of the Bible; and with an earthly paradise similar to the heavenly one. Prayer is all of these.

Line 14b, "something understood."

Note that this is the only line in which a semicolon is used to divide the thoughts within a line. This phrase, then, is separated more strongly from not only the phrase before it but perhaps from all the phrases before. The phrase, therefore, sets by itself and gains heightened importance. In that light, it could mean that prayer ultimately is something that goes beyond words and description and suggestion. It is something understood from the experience of it, not something adequately described by words. It could also mean that prayer is something understood by God. Another possibility is that, in prayer, we come to understand "something," something such as God, ourselves, and the nature of our journey.

The Parts of the Picture Come Together

All of the above information is an examination of each of the individual phrases of the poem. One must also look at the poem as a whole. The following comments are designed to provide perspective about the broader elements of the poem that unite it.

1. The most obvious unifying factor is prayer. Every phrase is a comment on it, or put another way, a suggestion concerning it.

2. Although it does not readily conform to the usual expectations of a sonnet, its structure gains unity from use of the sonnet form. Note the movement in the first eight lines. It begins with the somewhat tranquil images of "Church's banquet" and "angels age," then builds in lines 2-4 with more active images (breath returning, soul in paraphrase, heart in pilgrimage, and plummet sounding), then intensifies in lines 4-6 with forceful images of an engine, thunder, and a spear, and then modifies with the reduced tone of musical imagery in lines 7-8 (transposing and tune). The next six lines are filled with images elevated in tone and substance, images all "beyond the ordinary" (softness; peace; joy; love; bliss; gladness; exalted manna; heaven, which is ironically "in ordinary"; beyond the stars; and land of spices). In short, the poem moves through a myriad of images varying in intensity and tone but presented orderly within the movement of the two main divisions of the poem.

1. There are the feeding and blood images with Eucharistic overtones throughout (lines 1, 6, 10, and 13). The idea of union with God in prayer and in the Eucharist is thereby tied together and reinforced.

2. Biblical allusions are replete as they undergird and thereby unify the poem (two in line 1 and one each in lines 2, 5, 6, 7, 10, 13, and 14).

Reflections

1. What does the poem have to say about relationship with God?
2. What spiritual direction does it provide?
3. Which of the poet's descriptions of prayer are most helpful to you?
4. Which descriptions opened new thoughts to you?
5. How would you define prayer? What would you add to the poet's descriptions?
6. What effect does the poem have on your understanding of prayer?
7. Will it affect your prayer life?

Scriptures for further reflection:

See scripture references in the commentary on the poem.

THE STORM

If as the winds and waters here below
        Do fly and flow,
My sighs and tears as busy were above;
        Sure they would move
And much affect thee, as tempestuous times   5
Amaze poor mortals, and object their crimes.

Stars have their storms, even in a high degree,
        As well as we.
A throbbing conscience spurred by remorse
        Hath a strange force: 10
It quits the earth, and mounting more and more
Dares to assault thee, and besiege thy door.

There it stands knocking, to thy music's wrong,
        And drowns the song.
Glory and honor are set by, till it   15
        An answer get.
Poets have wronged poor storms: such days are best;
They purge the air without, within the breast.

The Big Picture

Jesus spoke of a persistent, aggressive kind of prayer (see the parables in Luke 11:5-9 and 18:1-8). Herbert alludes to this aspect of prayer in *Prayer (I)* when he characterizes prayer as an "Engine against th' Almighty" and "Reversed thunder." In this poem he continues in that vein by using storm imagery to describe prayer. Usually a storm is thought of as violence coming down from heaven, but here the storm is violence rising heavenward in the form of prayer (see Matthew 11:12 for a possible connection). The speaker compares his "sighs and tears" and his "throbbing conscience" to the "wind and waters" of a storm that "much affect" God as they dare to besiege His door with knocking.

The Parts of the Picture

Stanza 1. If the speaker's sighs and tears in his prayers "fly and flow" above as do the "winds and waters" of a storm "here below," they would move and affect God as "tempestuous times/ Amaze poor mortals" and "object" or disapprove of their sins or "crimes."

Stanza 2. The storm imagery continues. Stars, like humans, have their storms on high with meteor showers. Then the storm imagery shifts back to earth, concentrated in a "throbbing conscience spurred by remorse." In short, the speaker's prayer (the "sighs and tears" of line 3) is indeed a storm driven by the "strange force" of a "throbbing conscience" so powerful that it "quits the earth" and "dares to assault" God's door.

Stanza 3. The throbbing conscience stands at God's door as its knocking "wrongs" or disturbs the harmony of God's music (the harmony of the music of the spheres?). Praise of God's "Glory and honor" is set aside until an answer is given to the knocking. Then the concluding couplet shifts the focus. What is the good of all this storming of God's door? Is the knocking answered? We are not told. But we are told of the benefit of storms and, implicitly, of prayers that are like storms: they purge the air, within and without.

The Parts of the Picture Come Together

The series of images in the poem build to a climax with increasing intensity and then are calmed with the purging of the concluding couplet. Each image provides a comparison, and two images are paired within each stanza.

First, winds and waters of earthly storms are compared to the sighs and tears of the speaker. As the force of storms (their flying and flowing of winds and waters) have tempestuous effects, so, too, the sighs and tears of the speaker have a powerful effect on God. The basic imagery of the poem is established—the lament of the speaker is akin to an earthly storm in both its nature and effect.

The next pair of images retain the intensity of the storm and elevate it. First, the storm imagery is restated but this time as "Stars that have their storms." This "higher degree" of star storms is combined with the image of a human force, the strange force of a throbbing conscience that assaults and besieges heaven's doors. Thus, the sighs and tears of prayer now take on the elevated intensity of an assault on heaven.

The effects of the assault are detailed in the next image—the knocking on heaven's door, the disturbing and drowning out of heaven's music, and the forestalling of any talk of God's glory and honor until an answer to the knocking is given. The storm has reached its peak. Surely the doors will be opened.

But not so. In the imagery of the final two lines, the intensity is purged. Poets are wrong about storms. The best days are the stormy ones because of their purging effect "without, within the breast." The storm—one image—has led somewhat unexpectedly to the purge—the climactic image. It is an ending, a resolution, not without an element of surprise. The final effect of the storm—that is, the effect of the prayer of sighs and tears and of the remorseful, driven conscience—is not that the doors of heaven are opened, either forcefully or otherwise. The effect of the storm is purging. The storm is broken. Indeed the intensity of the entire poem is resolved. Now there is internal peace, external calm. This is the answer that prayer brings. Quite an answer!

And is not all of this somewhat related to the experience of Jesus at Gethsemane—with the storm of "take this cup from me" being resolved by the purging submission of " not my will but thine be done"?

Reflections

1. What does this poem have to say about relationship with God?
2. What spiritual direction does it provide?
3. How would you characterize your prayers? Bold, like a storm? Timid, hesitating? Both? Otherwise?
4. How do you respond to the idea of prayer as a storm? Does this poem provide insights into prayer that may help your prayer life? If so, how?
5. How do you respond to the way in which the poem is resolved in the final two lines with the shift of the imagery to that of purging? How do you respond to the idea that the answer to prayer is sometimes found in the process of praying (that is, in the purging effect on the one doing the praying)? Is that enough of an answer?

Scriptures for further reflection:
Genesis 18:22-33
Matthew 11:12
Luke 11:5-9
Luke 18:1-8

THE METHOD

Poor heart, lament.
For since thy God refuseth still,
There is some rub, some discontent,
    Which cools his will.

    Thy Father could   5
Quickly effect, what thou dost move;
For he is Power: and sure he would;
    For he is Love.

    Go search this thing,
Tumble thy breast, and turn thy book.   10
If thou hadst lost a glove or ring,
    Wouldst thou not look?

    What do I see
Written above there? Yesterday
I did behave me carelessly,   15
    When I did pray.

    And should God's ear
To such indifferents chained be,
Who do not their own motions hear?
    Is God less free?   20

    But stay! what's there?
Late when I would have something done,
I had a motion to forbear,
    Yet I went on.

    And should God's ear,   25
Which needs not man, be tied to those
Who hear not him, but quickly hear
    His utter foes?

Then once more pray:

Down with thy knees, up with thy voice.   30

Seek pardon first, and God will say,

Glad heart rejoice.

The Big Picture

In many of Herbert's poems, the speaker directs his thoughts to God prayerfully. In this poem, the speaker directs his thoughts to himself. The thoughts concern the correct method of prayer. As in *Denial*, the speaker experiences separation from God. Unlike *Denial*, however, this poem turns into a prayer of confession and a call to repentance. In short, the correct method of prayer is to examine one's life first and seek pardon for sins discovered.

The Parts of the Picture

Stanzas 1-3. As is often the case in Herbert's poetry, the problem is defined early on. The elements of the problem are threefold: God refuses to hear the prayer of the speaker; his heart laments; and the reason for God's refusal is that there is some "rub," something that has cooled His will or desire to listen. The problem is not with God since He "is Power" and could "Quickly effect" what the speaker wants, and surely He would since He "is Love," also. The problem, therefore, must be with the speaker. The first step in resolving the problem is for the speaker to examine himself by searching the pages of his book of life. After all, if he had lost a possession, would he not search for it?

Stanza 4-7. The first discovery in his search is indifference, or behaving carelessly, as he prays. Should God's ear "be chained to" the "motions" (or petitions) of those who are indifferent to their own requests? There is yet a second discovery—a failure by the speaker to respond appropriately to a "notion to forebear." Should God hear those who do not listen to Him?

Stanza 8. Having realized these failings in his own life, the speaker is now ready to pray. The key is to "Seek pardon first." God's response will call for joy.

The Parts of the Picture Come Together

This is another rendition of Herbert's theme that the way to approach God is with a "broken and contrite heart." The poem also dares to give a reason for God's silence (often, as in *Denial*, God's silence is a mystery). Here the problem is with the speaker, not God. Here, rather than extended lament, there are confession and repentance. Here the proper method of prayer is given—confession comes before petition.

All of this is done within a soliloquy that re-enacts "the method" in three parts in which the reader is able to experience the method itself. First, the problem is defined—separation from God. And the speaker is the cause of the problem. This is the first step of "the method"—confessing that the cause of the problem is within one's self. Then there is follow-through. Self-examination is the solution with the speaker's reviewing the pages of the book of his life and discovering, in a most personal fashion, specific examples of his sins. Finally, he is ready to pray, seeking pardon first, and confident of God's response.

Reflections

1. What does this poem have to say about relationship with God?
2. What spiritual direction does it provide?
3. The poem does not make the claim that God's silence is always caused by man's sin, but it does propose that man's sin can be the cause of God's silence. How does that truth play out in your life?
4. The poem provides two examples of the speaker's failings in his prayer life— behaving carelessly or indifferently in prayer and asking for something despite having an inclination to refrain from asking for it.

   What is there in your prayer life that may lead to God's "discontent" with, or "coolness of will" toward, your prayers?

Scriptures for further reflection:

Psalm 51

MATTENS

I cannot open mine eyes,
But thou art ready there to catch
My morning-soul and sacrifice:
Then we must needs for that day make a match.

My God, what is a heart?   5
Silver, or gold, or precious stone,
Or star, or rainbow, or a part
Of all these things, or all of them in one?

My God, what is a heart,
That thou should it so eye, and woo,   10
Pouring upon it all thy art,
As if that thou had nothing else to do?

Indeed man's whole estate
Amounts (and richly) to serve thee:
He did not heaven and earth create,   15
Yet studies them, not him by whom they be.

Teach me thy love to know;
That this new light, which now I see,
May both the work and workman show:
Then by a sun-beam I will climb to thee.   20

The Big Picture

What are your first thoughts upon awakening in the morning? Perhaps they turn to upcoming activities for the day or to lingering thoughts of yesterday. This poem is a morning prayer, and the speaker's thoughts go directly toward God. His thoughts are wide ranging—from finding God "ready" for him as he awakens, to marveling at God's attention to man, to disappointment at man's paying more attention to the creation than to the Creator, and back to his love relationship with God. But the poem is also tied together. All of it concerns the relationship of the poet, and mankind, with God.

The Parts of the Picture

Stanza 1 sets the scene. God is "ready" "to catch" the speaker's awakening being ("soul") and activity ("sacrifice"). This is is the time for God and the speaker to make "a match" for the day.

Stanzas 2- 3 expand the scope of the poem from the relationship of God and the speaker to that of God and mankind. Both stanzas are composed of questions. The question of stanza 2 concerns the nature of a heart where the vital connection with God is made. Is a heart one or all or part of the things listed in this stanza? Stanza 3 goes beyond the question of defining a heart to the larger inquiry of why God is interested in the heart. Echoing Psalm 8:4 ("what is man that thou art mindful of him"), the poet contemplates the reason for God's eyeing and wooing the heart and pouring out all His "art" upon it.

Stanza 4 is a kind of brief lament, almost an aside. As the speaker expands the subject to "man's whole estate," there are two declarations. The first concerns the purpose of man's estate (lines 13-14) which is to serve God. The other (lines 15-16) heads in the opposite direction as it comments on man's inadequate response to God as man spends his time studying the creation rather than the Creator.

Rather than follow this topic of inadequate response, the speaker returns in **stanza 5** to the beauty of his relationship with God. He petitions God for guidance on how to experience God's love so that the "new light" of this day will reveal both creation ("work") and Creator ("workman") and serve to unite the speaker with God. With the image of the poet's ascent to God on a sunbeam, the poem concludes, as it began, with a simple and profound image of the relationship of the speaker and God.

The Parts of the Picture Come Together

This poem begins with the intimacy and readiness that are at the core of the relationship of the speaker and God. The speaker's focus is not on the demands of the unfolding day nor is his focus on his desire for God to help him meet those demands. Instead, the speaker's focus is on the present moment with God who is ready for him as he opens his eyes. This is a time for the speaker and his God to "make a match."

The movement then becomes one of contemplative questioning. What is the nature of a heart. More importantly, why should God take such great interest in it? As the contemplation continues, there is a touch of sadness as the speaker realizes that, despite God's creation of and interest in His creature, man—whose whole purpose is to serve God—chooses instead to study creation rather than the Creator.

Then the speaker corrects his course. He has been distracted (as all of us are in our morning prayers) as he has wandered away from his present moment with God to thoughts about the failures of man. Now he returns to the beauty of this morning moment with God. His prayer now becomes a petition as he requests that God will teach him of His love so that the morning light will show him both creation and the Creator. He concludes with the image of climbing to God on the sunbeam of the new day, an image that subtly and brilliantly completes the union of creature and Creator with which the poem began.

Reflections

1. What does this poem tell us about relationship with God?
2. What spiritual direction does it provide?
3. How would you describe your morning prayer? Does the poem reflect any dimension of prayer that you would like to add to your morning prayer?
4. In what ways do the revelations of the natural world lead you to God? Or is your relation to the natural world an end in itself rather than a means of reflecting on your relationship with God?

Scriptures for further reflection:

Psalm 5:3
Psalm 30:5
Psalm 59:16
Isaiah 33:2
Lamentations 3:22-23
Mark 1:35
Romans 1:21-25

EVENSONG

Blest be the God of love,
Who gave me eyes, and light, and power this day,
Both to be busy, and to play.
But much more blest be God above,
Who gave me sight alone, 5
Which to himself he did deny:
For when he sees my ways, I die:
But I have got his son, and he has none.

What have I brought thee home
For this thy love? have I discharged the debt, 10
Which this day's favour did beget?
I ran; but all I brought, was foam.
Thy diet, care, and cost
Do end in bubbles, balls of wind;
Of wind to thee whom I have crossed 15
But balls of wild-fire to my troubled mind.

Yet still thou goest on,
And now with darkness closes weary eyes,
Saying to man, It doth suffice:
Henceforth repose; your work is done. 20
Thus in thy ebony box
Thou dost enclose us, till the day
Put our amendment in our way,
And give new wheels to our disordered clocks.

I muse, which shows more love, 25
The day or night: that is the gale, this the harbour;
That is the walk, and this the arbour;
Or that the garden, this the grove.
My God, thou art all love.
Not one poor minute scapes thy breast, 30
But brings a favour from above;
And in this love, more than in the bed, I rest.

The Big Picture

As the speaker examines the completed day, he moves from thanksgiving, to confession, back to thanksgiving, to introspective musing, and back to thanksgiving full of praise and peace. In the passing of the day and in the coming darkness, the poet sees God at work—loving, forgiving, and restoring.

The Parts of the Picture

Stanza 1. The poem opens with thanksgiving. The first three lines of stanza 1 mention specific gifts given that day by "the God of love." Line 4 is addressed to the "God above" and introduces the theme of confession. Lines 4-7 echo Psalm 130:3, "If thou, Lord, shouldest mark iniquities, O Lord, who shall stand?" Thanksgiving, in effect, is given for God's "blindness" (line 6) to the poet's failures of that day. A somewhat indirect way into the theme of forgiveness is introduced in line 8 with a reference to the poet's having God's son (and thereby forgiveness) and God "hath none." Possibly this is an allusion to God's giving his son as stated in John 3:16. In any case, these opening stanzas have introduced both the poet's gratitude for, and his failures of, the day. The subject of his failures is developed in the next two stanzas.

Stanza 2 is a confession. Lines 9-11 are questions about what the poet has done in response to the love given him this day. Lines 12-16 contain the answer in a confession of failures. To describe these failures, he notes his effort ("I ran") but then points out that his results lack substance, being only "foam," "bubbles," "balls of winds." In his own guilty mind, these failures are "balls of wildfire."

In **stanza 3**, there is a return to the theme of thanksgiving as the speaker describes God's reaction to the failures. God simply goes on, speaking words of comfort as He "closes weary eyes." Lines 21-24 describe the restoration that the night ("thy ebony box") brings. This restoration is portrayed through the metaphor of night being an ebony box which renders harmless poisonous liquids. With the new day there will be improvement ("amendment") that is likened to "disordered clocks" receiving "new wheels."

In **stanza 4** the speaker muses upon the question of which shows more love, the day or the night. The day is a "gale," the night a "harbor": the day is "the walk," the night the "arbor"; and the day is "the garden," the night "the grove." The poem concludes with a praise of God's love in which the poet finds his true "rest."

The Parts of the Picture Come Together

When and where do we learn about the nature of God? This poem speaks of finding the nature of God at the end of a day. First, God is the "God of love" who has been encountered in the just-completed day, the God who has given "eyes, light, and power" for the day's work and play. But, more than that, He is the "God above," the forgiving

God who chooses to be blind to the failures of the speaker, the giving God who has given His only son.

The speaker then turns to himself, but only as a way of commenting further on the nature of God. The speaker's actions of the day have been an example of failed stewardship of the day's gifts. And what is God's response to man's failures? He is the undaunted God of great faithfulness, the God who comforts man by closing his weary eyes and by renewing him with the enclosure of the night. The speaker is left musing about which is the greater gift, the day or the night.

The "God of love" at the beginning of the poem becomes the "God of all love" by the end. The poem is the unfolding of the speaker's discovery of the nature of God. The speaker has found God by looking back, in finding the manifestation of God's power and love in the events of the day, in experiencing God's forgiveness in the midst of the disappointment of his own failures, in comforting words after work is done, in the restorative powers of God's night, in the favors that always flow, in the rest greater than that found in any bed. It is quite a discovery.

Reflections

1. What does this poem tell us about relationship with God?
2. What spiritual direction does it provide?
3. How important is an evening prayer? What are some of the functions it can serve?
4. Does the poem help you in seeing a way of talking to God at the end of the day? Is it helpful in influencing your thoughts about what an evening prayer should be?

Scriptures for further reflection:

Psalm 3:5
Psalm 4:8
Psalm 63:6-8
Matthew 11:28-30

SPECIAL BLESSINGS OF THE CHURCH

*T*hese poems are about special blessings associated with the church. As a priest in the Church of England, Herbert valued immensely the sacrament of the Eucharist. There are many references to it throughout his poetry. Here are two poems devoted exclusively to the Eucharist (*The Banquet* and *The Invitation*). Although the third poem, *The Bunch of Grapes*, is not exclusively concerned with the Eucharist, it is an example of Herbert's use of it in a larger context. The fourth poem is a song of praise to another one of Herbert's special church blessings: *Church Music*.

THE BANQUET

Welcome sweet and sacred cheer,
              Welcome dear;
With me, in me, live and dwell:
For thy neatness passeth sight,
              Thy delight   5
Passeth tongue to taste or tell.

O what sweetness from the bowl
              Fills my soul,
Such as is, and makes divine!
Is some star (fled from the sphere)   10
              Melted there,
As we sugar melt in wine?

Or hath sweetness in the bread
              Made ahead
To subdue the smell of sin;   15
Flowers, and gums, and powders giving
              All their living,
Lest the Enemy should win?

Doubtless, neither star nor flower
              Hath the power   20
Such a sweetness to impart:
Only God, who gives perfumes,
              Flesh assumes,
And with it perfumes my heart.

But as Pomanders and wood   25
              Still are good,
Yet being bruised are better scented:
God, to show how far his love
              Could improve,
Here, as broken, is presented.   30

When I had forgot my birth,

             And on earth

In delights of earth was drowned;

God took blood, and needs would be

             Spilt with me,   35

And so found me on the ground.

Having raised me to look up,

             In a cup

Sweetly he doth meet my taste.

But I still being low and short,   40

             Far from court,

Wine becomes a wing at last.

For with it alone I fly

             To the sky:

Where I wipe mine eyes, and see   45

What I seek, for what I sue;

             Him I view,

Who hath done so much for me.

Let the wonder of his pity

             Be my ditty,   50

And take up my lines and life:

Hearken under pain of death,

             Hands and breath;

Strive in this, and love the strife.

The Big Picture

Whereas *The Invitation* encourages the reader to partake in communion, *The Banquet* reveals the speaker's experience of the Eucharist. This experience is likened to a banquet with its elements and effects described.

The Parts of the Picture

Stanza 1. This is both a welcome to the "sweet and sacred cheer" of the Eucharist and an invitation for it to continue to "live and dwell" with and in the speaker for its benefits are unsurpassed and inexplicable.

Stanza 2. The sweetness and effect of the wine are described with the mention of the possibility of a star falling from its sphere and melting in the wine to provide its divine effect.

Stanza 3. The bread is considered. The stanza is a rhetorical question which focuses on the sweetness of the bread having "made a head" (or gathered in opposition) to "subdue the smell of sin" with "flowers, gums, and powders" also giving "All their living" to this effort against the Enemy.

Stanza 4. Neither stars nor flowers could produce the sweetness of the Eucharist; only the presence of God can give such "perfumes."

Stanza 5. God is indeed present—but in a special way. It is His "broken presence," alluding to the shed blood and broken body. This brokenness is compared to Pomanders (containers with aromatic substances) and wood that are "better scented" when "bruised." Hence, the brokenness of God in the Eucharist is a sign of the extension of His love, improved "Here, as broken."

Stanza 6. Now the speaker turns to his own brokenness. It was in his brokenness (the speaker had forgotten his heavenly origin by being drowned in "delights of earth") that God "spilt" His blood to meet the needs of the speaker as He found him on the ground in a fallen state.

Stanzas 7- 8. The wine becomes a wing and raises the speaker from his fallen state. Continuing in stanza 8 with the metaphor of the wine as a wing, the speaker ascends to God.

Stanza 9. All of this leads to a pledge of devotion. It is the "wonder" of God's pity that is to be the speaker's "ditty" or the theme of the "lines and life" of the speaker. Under "pain of death" his "Hands and breath" are to strive in this endeavor and to "love the strife."

The Parts of the Picture Come Together

To be sure, God's presence is in the Eucharist for Herbert. But there is more. First, there is undiminished joy, beginning with the opening welcome. Then come the petition, the description of the elements, the brokenness of God, and the brokenness and conversion of the speaker. And all this culminates in the speaker's dedication of his "lines and life" to strive to write of this wonder of God's pity—and love doing it!

It all begins with the focused elevation of the Eucharist contained in the opening welcome. With the poem entitled *The Banquet*, one would expect an opening welcome to the guests. But not so here. Instead, it is the Eucharist that is welcomed with a petition for it to indwell the speaker with its elegance.

Then come the elements. First, there is the sweetness of the wine associated with the divine and compared to a star fallen from a heavenly sphere and "melted there." And there is the bread that subdues the Enemy of sin. A most important further presence is in the Eucharist. Only God could impart such a sweetness. But He comes in a special way. It is the brokenness of God that is here, reflecting the blood and the wine and the brokenness of the bread and body. As pomanders and wood "being bruised are better scented," God is able "to show how far his love/ Could improve; / Here as broken." Herein is the great irony of the Christian faith— that God's nature is shown most fully in the brokenness of the Son. Indeed in stanza 5 the poem reaches the high point of the description of the Banquet.

But the poem has not reached its climax. To do that, it must move to and through the effects of the Eucharist on the speaker. With stanza 6, the poem begins that movement. The journey of the speaker reached its lowest when he "on earth/ In delights of earth was drowned." Through His spilled blood, God found the speaker "on the ground," and through the cup, "Wine becomes a wing at last," carrying him to see God.

The speaker's ascent to God is certainly near the climax of the poem. But it is on earth, with the surrender and dedication of the speaker's "lines and life" to the wonder of God's grace, that the greatest effect of the Eucharist takes place. It is the redemptive deliverance of the experience of God's mercy embodied in the Eucharist that gives direction and commitment to the speaker's "lines and life." To declare the wonder of all this will be his theme. To strive to do this and to love the strife will be his life.

Reflections

1. What does the poem have to say about relationship with God?
2. What spiritual direction does it provide?
3. How do you react to the poet's portrayal of the Eucharist? Are there any points of connection for you?
4. If you were to describe your experiences with the Eucharist (or Communion or the Lord's Supper), how would you do it? In this poem, the poet uses the image of a banquet to provide the setting for portraying his experiences.
   Is there an image you would use to assist in describing your experiences?

Scriptures for further reflection:

John 6:48-59
I Corinthians 11:23-28

THE INVITATION

Come ye hither All, whose taste
                Is your waste;
Save your cost, and mend your fare.
God is here prepared and drest,
                And the feast,   5
God, in whom all dainties are.

Come ye hither All, whom wine
                Doth define,
Naming you not to your good:
Weep what ye have drunk amiss,   10
                And drink this,
Which before ye drink is blood.

Come ye hither All, whom pain
                Doth arraign,
Bringing all your sins to sight: 15
Taste and fear not: God is here
                In this cheer,
And on sin doth cast the fright.

Come ye hither All, whom joy
                Doth destroy,   20
While ye graze without your bounds:
Here is joy that drowneth quite
                Your delight,
As a flood the lower grounds.

Come ye hither All, whose love   25
                Is your dove,
And exalts you to the sky:
Here is love, which having breath
                Even in death,
After death can never die.   30

Lord I have invited all,

> And I shall

Still invite, still call to thee:

For it seems but just and right

> In my sight, 35

Where is All, here All should be.

The Big Picture

This poem issues a call to "All" to come to communion. Each stanza preceding the final one contains an invitation to a different group based on the needs of each group. In the final stanza, the speaker tells the Lord of his invitation and the reason for it.

The Parts of the Picture

Stanza 1. Here is an invitation to those "whose taste is your waste" or those whose desires are barren, spent, expended. Line 3 is reminiscent of Isaiah 55:1-2 which calls for those without money to come to drink of "the waters" "without money, and without price." Thus, the invitation is without cost or a fare (or "fare" could also be translated "food" or "travel" and the invitation could be to "mend" or make whole these). And the reward is great: God is prepared as the feast. This could be an indication of Herbert's belief in the Real Presence or that God is present in the Eucharist.

Stanza 2. The invitation is to those who are defined or characterized by drinking wine "amiss" and thereby earning a bad reputation for it. They are to "weep" or repent for their misuse of wine and turn to the wine that is the blood of Christ.

Stanza 3. The invitation is to those who are arraigned or indicted by the pain of their sins. These people can "taste and fear not" since forgiveness is here in God's cheer which frightens sin.

Stanza 4. Two kinds of joy are contrasted. First, there is the joy that destroys those who "graze" or wander with no confining boundaries. Apparently this is destructive joy arising from aimless wandering. The invitation is to another kind of joy, a joy that "drowneth quite/ Your delight." This is done in a manner similar to the improvement of lower lands by the occasional flooding of them. Hence, this is a joy that restores or improves with its quiet manner of submerging delight.

Stanza 5. This is an invitation to those who fly or ascend on love. In the Eucharist these people will experience a love that has a greater ascent, meaning that in death it still has breath and thereby never dies.

Stanza 6. The speaker addresses the Lord. He reports what he has done and will do. He has invited "all" to the Eucharist since "All" should be where "All" is.

The Parts of the Picture Come Together

Methodically the speaker works through the invitation to the Eucharist. For each group to whom an invitation is issued, the invitation is designed to meet the greatest need of those invited. For those whose taste is wasted or spent, a feast of "dainties" is promised. For those who have drunken wine amiss, there is a beckoning to turn from that kind of foolish drinking to the drinking of the wine of the Eucharist. For those arraigned by the pain of their sins, these are told to fear not and to experience the cheer of God's casting out of sin. For those destroyed by the joy of aimless wandering, the joy of a drowning that restores or improves is promised. And for those who ascend on love, a love even greater is available in the Eucharist since it soars beyond death.

For the speaker, the Eucharist supplies all deficiencies. In it is "All," the experience of God, and therefore the invitation is to all. It is an invitation to something not attained by human effort. In short, it is God's answer to man's deficiencies. And as the deficiencies extend to all, so the invitation is to All.

Reflections

1. What does the poem have to say about relationship with God?
2. What spiritual direction does it provide?
3. How do you react to the author's invitation list? What other people would you include?
4. If you were sending out an invitation for people to attend the Eucharist or Communion or Lord's Supper, what reasons would you give for their participating in the event?

Scriptures for further reflection:

Psalm 34:8
Matthew 22:1-10
Luke 14:15-24

THE BUNCH OF GRAPES

Joy, I did lock thee up: but some bad man
        Hath let thee out again:
And now, me thinks, I am where I began
        Seven years ago: one vogue and vein,
        One air of thoughts usurps my brain.   5
I did towards Canaan draw; but now I am
Brought back to the Red Sea, the sea of shame.

For as the Jews of old by God's command
        Traveled, and saw no town;
So now each Christian hath his journeys spanned: 10
        Their story pens and sets us down.
        A single deed is small renown.
God's works are wide, and let in future times;
His ancient justice overflows our crimes.

Then have we too our guardian fires and clouds;   15
        Our Scripture-dew drops fast:
We have our sands and serpents, tents and shrouds;
        Alas! our murmurings come not last.
        But where's the cluster? Where's the taste
Of mine inheritance? Lord, if I must borrow,   20
Let me as well take up their joy, as sorrow.

But can he want the grape, who hath the wine?
        I have their fruit and more.
Blessed be God, who prospered Noah's vine,
        And made it bring forth grapes good store.   25
        But much more him I must adore,
Who of the Law's sour juice sweet wine did make,
Even God himself being pressed for my sake.

The Big Picture

The speaker, at a time when joy has abandoned him, finds instruction from the Old Testament story of the "bunch of grapes" in Numbers 13. He sees his story within the context of that biblical story and concludes that his present joy is to be found in something far greater than the grapes of the biblical story. It is found in the Eucharist made possible by Christ's sacrifice.

The Parts of the Picture

The Biblical Background. At the heart of the poem is the story found in Numbers 13. Those sent by Moses to spy on the land and people of Canaan cut a cluster of grapes (v. 23) to show the fruit of the land. But the joy of the discovery of these grapes was lost when the spies brought back a fearful report on the power of the people of Canaan, and the Hebrews decided not to enter the land. It is in this story that the speaker finds the instruction that enables him to find joy in the "wine" of his current situation. There are also biblical references to the story of the Jews wandering in the wilderness after being delivered from Egypt (see lines 8-9 of the poem and Exodus 16 ff), and to Noah's vine (Genesis 9:20-27) being redeemed (lines 24-25 of the poem).

Stanza 1. This is a lament about the speaker's present situation. Joy has escaped him, and he has returned to where he was seven years before as one "vogue and vein" (or of a fashionable and general tendency with one kind of thought in his mind). He was headed toward Canaan (the Promised Land) but now finds himself "brought back to the Red Sea, the sea of shame." Why the Red Sea is a "sea of shame" or what has caused joy to escape him is unclear, but his present disappointment is strikingly clear. These references to the Red Sea and Canaan are the first connection with the story of the deliverance of God's people from Egypt and their subsequent wanderings in the wilderness toward Canaan. It is this story that comes to the forefront in stanzas 2 and 3 as the speaker works through the problem stated in stanza 1.

Stanza 2. The journey of the "Jews of old by God's command" is similar to the journey of the Christian in the speaker's day. As the Jew's story was at God's command, so too each Christian's journey is "spann'd" or measured. Their story of old provides the context for understanding the present moment of the speaker's journey. God's works are "wide" and His "ancient justice overflows our crimes." The reference to "crimes" may tie in with the loss of joy and the sea of shame of stanza 1.

Stanza 3. The analogy with the past becomes more specific. Like the "Jews of old," Christians have God's "guardian fires and clouds" (see Exodus 13:21), "Scripture-dew" or feedings (see Exodus 16:14-15), and the experience of "sands and serpents, tents and shrouds" and murmurings along the way of their journey. In line 19, there is a shift from similarities to contrast. The Jews had their cluster of grapes, their taste of inheritance from the Promised Land, but where is this for the speaker? If his journey is like the Jew's, and he experiences their sorrow, why does he not experience their joy, also? Where is his cluster of grapes? The answer is to be found in stanza 4.

Stanza 4. The answer is in Christ's sacrifice and in the wine of the Eucharist made possible by that sacrifice. In having this wine, the speaker has more than the Jews of old. The poem, which began with a lament, ends with two bursts of praise in lines 24-28. First, "Blessed be God" who redeemed "Noah's vine." Here the vine symbolizes Israel's past. It is the vine that Noah began and misused (see Genesis 9:20-21), that was planted and then broken (See Psalm 80:8-19), and that was finally redeemed by Jesus, the true vine (see John 15:1). The concluding praise (lines 26-28) centers on this true vine who, as "God himself, being pressed for my sake," transformed the "sour juice" of the Law into the "sweet wine" of the Eucharist.

The Parts of the Picture Come Together

The force that drives this poem is that of problem solving. It is a particular kind of problem solving that starts with the despair of the self in the present moment and then moves beyond self to God's greatest gift. Something has gone wrong on the speaker's journey, and we know not what. But we do know its effects—lack of joy and loss of progress coupled with backward movement and shame. To whom or what is the speaker to turn? It is to scripture that the speaker turns, specifically to the journey of the "Jews of old." This connection enables him to work on his present problem within the larger perspective of the workings of God rather than merely within his "single deed." And so the first major movement of the poem opens as the speaker is able to come outside the despair of his own self and into the hope found in Scripture.

In this opening up, the speaker recognizes the similarities between his journey and that of the "Jews of old." But the significant problem remains. While the Jews of old found their joy, their inheritance of the cluster of grapes from the Promised Land, the speaker has not found his. Or so he thinks. In a quick turn (from line 21 to 22) the poem opens further as it makes its second and climactic movement, a movement that truly resolves the problem stated in the beginning. It is a movement from Old to New Testament, from Noah's vine to the true vine of Jesus, from the Law's "sour juice" to "sweet wine" of the Eucharist. This movement comes in the speaker's realization that he has more than a cluster of grapes. Indeed, he has the wine from the grapes, a sweet wine made by God himself being pressed for the speaker's sake.

The movement of the poem has begun with the small world of the speaker's lack of joy and opened into the large world of Scripture and God's workings. It opens even further as the poem culminates in the true vine sacrificed to make sweet wine. Gone is the speaker's lack of joy; present is the cup of salvation.

Reflections

1. What does this poem have to say about relationship with God?

2. What spiritual direction does it provide?

3. In the background of this poem is the exhortation of Paul the Apostle to the Corinthians to be instructed by the story of God's workings with the "Jews of old" (see I Corinthians 10:1-13, especially verses 11-13). In short, the speaker resolves his problem by examining it within the larger context of the biblical story. How do you respond to this as a method of problem solving, as a method of using Scriptures? What are the advantages and or disadvantages to this approach?

4. What biblical stories are there that may be helpful in resolving problems you are currently working through?

5. In the poem the speaker asks for grapes and then realizes that God has provided him with wine that is greater than grapes. Do you ever find yourself asking God for one thing only to discover that He has already provided you with something far greater?

Scriptures for further reflection:

See Scripture references in the commentary and reflections above.

Church Music

Sweetest of sweets, I thank you: when displeasure
      Did through my body wound my mind,
You took me thence, and in your house of pleasure
      A dainty lodging me assigned.

Now I in you without a body move,   5
      Rising and falling with your wings:
We both together sweetly live and love,
      Yet say sometimes, God help poor Kings.

Comfort, I'll die; for if you post from me,
      Sure I shall do so, and much more: 10
But if I travel in your company,
      You know the way to heaven's door.

The Big Picture

George Herbert loved music. It was prominent throughout his life, as pointed out by Amy Charles, his foremost biographer: "Herbert loved music all his life, probably secular consort as well as sacred music; and all his life he sang, played, and perhaps even composed music."[73] Musicians visited his home; music was part of the curriculum at his boyhood school; he played both the lute and viol; and during his time as priest at Bemerton, he attended Evensong at nearby Salisbury Cathedral twice weekly to hear the singing men of Sarum. As he had requested, these singing men performed the service at his funeral.[74]

This love of music manifested itself in Herbert's poetry. Another of his biographers points out that "a quarter of his poems reflect his love of music, and the image of the untuned instrument is the one he most often applies to himself."[75] Although the poem *Church Music* does not portray the complete dimension that music played in Herbert's life, it does, in its brevity and playfulness, poignantly portray his deep love of church music. The poem begins with an expression of gratitude for the "house of pleasure" provided by church music; it continues with a description of the ecstasy Herbert experienced with this music; and it ends with the pronouncement that he will travel to "heaven's door" with music.

The Parts of the Picture

Stanza 1. The speaker characterizes church music as "Sweetest of sweets." In the remainder of stanza 1, he expresses gratitude that this music was able to take him out of the wounds of his body and mind and into a "house of pleasure."

Stanza 2. Here is described the ecstasy of a "rising and falling" on the wings of music. He and music, "sweetly" living and loving together, sometimes say a prayer for "poor Kings" who are confined to the mundane life of governing.

Stanza 3. The address to church music continues as the speaker declares that he will die if music "posts" from him (or leaves him), but if he travels with the music, it will take him to heaven's door.

The Parts of the Picture Come Together

The poem begins with a movement that runs throughout, a movement provided and accompanied by music, a movement out of the speaker and into something of immense pleasure. The first movement is from the displeasure of his wounded body and mind to his assigned lodging in music's "house of pleasure." The second occurs within that world of music—a "rising and falling" on the wings of music as together they "live and love." The poem concludes with a request for one final movement—a movement in the company of music to heaven's door. Joy, even eternal joy, is found outside the speaker in the gift of his assigned lodging in the world of music.

Reflections

1. This is a poem of sheer joy. The joy stems from the poet's coming out of himself and the ability of music to provide "a house of pleasure" for the poet as he does this. What does this have to say about relationship with God?
2. What spiritual direction does the poem provide?
3. This poem captures the praise of gratitude, the ecstasy of soaring and falling with church music, and the exuberant declaration of the desire to follow this music to heaven's door. Even if church music does not affect you as it did Herbert, is there anything in your life that provides comparable joy? How would you describe it?
4. If church music is a source of significant joy to you, what would you include in a poem of praise to it?

Scriptures for further reflection:

I Chronicles 15:15-16 and 19-22   Psalm 150

Nehemiah 12:27-29   Acts 16:25-28

Psalm 68:24-26   Colossians 3:15-17

Psalm 100   Revelation 5:9-14 and 15:1-4

More Insights

Dust to Dust (with lessons learned)
> *Church Monuments*

Rebellion (and submission)
> *The Collar*

Brevity (and living well)
> *Life*

Not Understanding the Ways of God and Self
> *Justice (I)*

Restlessness
> *The Pulley*

Anxiety and Living in the Present Moment
> *The Discharge*

God Within Us
> *Sion*

God the Architect
> *The Church Floor*

Poetry (and being with God)
> *The Quiddity*

The Bible
> *The Holy Scriptures (I)*

CHURCH MONUMENTS

While that my soul repairs to her devotion,
Here I intomb my flesh, that it betimes
May take acquaintance of this heap of dust;
To which the blast of death's incessant motion,
Fed with the exhalation of our crimes,   5
Drives all at last. Therefore I gladly trust
My body to this school, that it may learn
To spell his elements, and find his birth
Written in dusty heraldry and lines;
Which dissolution sure doth best discern,   10
Comparing dust with dust, and earth with earth.
These laugh at Jet and Marble put for signs,
To sever the good fellowship of dust,
And spoil the meeting. What shall point out them,
When they shall bow, and kneel, and fall down flat   15
To kiss those heaps, which now they have in trust?
        Dear flesh, while I do pray, learn here thy stem
And true descent; that when thou shalt grow fat,
And wanton in thy cravings, thou mayst know,
That flesh is but the glass, which holds the dust   20
That measures all our time; which also shall
Be crumbled into dust. Mark here below
How tame these ashes are, how free from lust,
That thou mayst fit thy self against thy fall.

The Big Picture

For centuries Christians have celebrated Ash Wednesday as the first day of the Lenten Season. It is a service emphasizing man's mortality and penitence, and its name derives from the priest imposing ashes on the forehead of each attendant with the words "Remember that you are dust and to dust you shall return." This poem is an Ash Wednesday poem in that it utilizes the image of dust to convey its message of our mortality.

The poem is a meditation. The setting is a church in which the tombstones are found inside the building.[76] The subject is the decay of all things into dust, including the "church monuments" (the grave markers) used to mark the sites of those buried. The poem is a "teaching moment," a composite of lessons to be learned by the speaker's flesh whose destiny is dust. It begins with the speaker's declaration that "here" (the cemetery) is the place where he will "entomb my flesh." It then moves through a description of the dissolution not only of the flesh but of the grave markers themselves. It concludes with a direct address to his flesh concerning the humbling lesson of the flesh's role in life (it is "the glass that holds the dust that measures all our time"). To be sure, the poem focuses on death but not for the sake of being morbid. Instead, the speaker uses death and the dissolution of the flesh as a means to provide instruction about how to live in light of our mortality.

The Parts of the Picture

Lines 1-6a. The poem begins with the speaker attending a church service as the speaker's "soul repairs to her devotion" (or returns to the devotion of the service) while he meditates on his flesh being entombed "here" in the church in the church when he dies.[77] In good time ("betimes") his flesh will make acquaintance with the "heap of dust" that awaits it in the cemetery. This is the first mention of dust, the controlling image of the poem, to which the poet returns explicitly six more times. It is to dust that all are driven by the exhaust "of our crimes" (or the sins or our fallen state). With the expansion of focus from "my flesh" in line 2 to "our" and "all" in lines 5 and 6, the speaker universalizes the concern of the poem. In short, the meditation is centered in the fate of the speaker's flesh, but the thoughts apply to "all flesh."

Lines 6b-11. The fact that the flesh's destiny is dust leads the poet to conclude ("therefore" in line 6) that he will "gladly trust" his "body to this school." The mention of "school" and "learn" in line 7 introduces the poem's concern with schooling and learning. In this "school" of the church monuments, his body will learn to "spell" or "spell out" or understand its elements and find its "birth" in the "dusty heraldry" (coat of arms) and genealogical lines stated by the grave markers. It is in the dust that the body will find both its origin (its "birth") and its essential nature (its "elements"). The poet, therefore, "gladly trusts" his body to the "school" of the cemetery, for it is in the dust there that the flesh can "best discern" or come to an understanding of its beginning and ending, comparing dust with dust and earth with earth.

Lines 12-16. With line 12 the focus shifts away from the poet's "flesh" to the "church monuments" or gravestones. Dust and earth "laugh at the Jet and Marble monuments" put there to mark individual grave sites and thereby "sever" the "fellowship of dust" and "spoil the meeting" of dust and earth in the cemetery (lines 12-14a). In short, death and decay remove distinctions as flesh becomes one common matter of dust in the dissolution that takes place in the cemetery. This point is carried farther in the question of lines 14b-16 which answers itself. Ironically, these "church monuments" (which are there to mark distinctions among the dead) themselves "shall bow, and kneel, and fall down flat" as they, too, fall prey to decay and "kiss" and become a part of the dust "heaps." Proud monuments and proud flesh suffer the same dissolution.

Lines 17-24. With line 17, a direct address to the poet's flesh begins and goes to the end of the poem. This is the climax and heart of the poem. As indicated earlier in line 7 with the reference to "this school" and "learn," the time in the cemetery is a most important teaching moment. The instruction of "this school" is now stated directly to "Dear flesh." It is the poet's prayer that his flesh will learn its "stem and true descent" (its beginning and end, dust to dust and earth to earth). To understand the beginning and end of all flesh is a lesson that will serve the body well when it becomes "wanton" (cruel or promiscuous or luxuriant) in its "cravings" (**lines 18-19**.) In short, the lesson to be learned in the cemetery is a guard against such wanton living. The flesh, after all, as indicated in the marvelous image of **lines 20b-22a**, is nothing more than an hourglass that holds the dust "That measures all our time" (but not our eternity) and that shall also "be crumbled into dust." **Lines 22b-24** conclude the address to the flesh (here perhaps to everyone or "all flesh"). The lesson for the flesh is to "mark here below" or to learn on this earth that the end of all flesh is found in the tameness of the ashes of this cemetery. It is a lesson that will enable a person "to fit thyself against thy fall." The concluding word "fall" has at least two meanings. On the one hand, it means one's death. It could also mean one's fall into the sin of vanity or pride. These two meanings work together in that the lesson to be learned by the flesh prepares it for both death and from falling into the sin of pride. Or put another way, the lesson to be learned in this "school" of the cemetery is to avoid pride and thereby prepare oneself for death. As Joseph Summers points out:

> The flesh can escape neither its measuring content [as an hourglass] nor its final goal [dissolution]. The knowledge it has gained may however, serve as a bridle to 'tame' its lust. The flesh may 'fit' itself 'against' its 'fall' in that, in preparation for its final dissolution, it may oppose ('fit thyself against') its 'fall' into pride and lust.[78]

The Parts of the Picture Come Together

The poem ends with the word "fall." It is an appropriate way to end since the movement within the poem is consistently falling. Here are several examples. The poem opens with the soul's ascent to "her devotion" in line 1, while the next thought is that of the poet's body "falling" or being "entombed" in the cemetery (line 2). "All" are driven "at last" to "this heap of dust" (lines 3-6). The lessons of "this school" are found in the "dissolution" of "dust with dust" (lines 6b-11). The church monuments, built to stand and mark, finally "bow, and kneel, and fall down flat." (lines 12-16). Flesh is but an hourglass holding the descent of our dust and will itself "crumble into dust" (lines 17-22a). Finally, the lesson in the concluding lines (lines 22b-24) is a lesson for "here below" and concerns how to fit oneself "against thy fall." In effect, Herbert has not only portrayed his message in the imagery of dust but has also embodied that message in the repetition of images of downward movement. Again Summers is most helpful in pointing out that:

> The movement and sound of the poem suggests the 'fall' of the flesh and
> the monuments and the dust in the glass. The fall is not precipitous; it is as slow
> as the gradual fall of the monuments, as the crumbling of glass, as the descent
> of the flesh from Adam into dust.[79]

But despite this emphasis on "fall," the poem is not meant to be a "downer." It is meant to be a learning experience as indicated by the references to "school" and "learn" in line 6 and the concluding admonitions for "Dear flesh" to "learn here" and "Mark here below." It is meant to teach the lessons of our mortality from a Christian perspective. These lessons are the warning against wantonness and pride and vanity. It warns that ultimate meaning or enduring fulfillment is not found in the flesh. It is an encouragement for the reader to live wisely, to "fit thyself against thy fall."

The structure of the poem is also of considerable interest in determining how its parts come together. Considering the structure of the great majority of Herbert's poetry, *Church Monuments* is most unusual as is noted by Summers: "Herbert characteristically considered his stanzas as inviolable architectural units. Each usually contained a complete thought, representing one unit in the logic of the 'argument,' and the great majority of his stanzas end with full stops."[80] In this poem, however, the thought pattern is not discernible from the stanza structure. All of this is to say that the structure of the poem itself functions to reflect the dissolution being described in the poem. There are no neat divisions or logical packages of thought. Instead, sentence upon sentence is unraveled with an unceasing focus on the decay of flesh and the lessons to be learned from that decay, as is so aptly described by Summers:

> The dissolution of the body and monuments is paralleled by the dissolution of
> the sentences and the stanzas....The sentences sift down through the
> rhyme-scheme skeleton of the stanzas like the sand through the glass; and
> the glass has already begun to crumble."[81]

Reflections

1. Although the poem does not mention God, does it have anything to say about relationship with God?
2. What spiritual direction does it provide?
3. For what reasons is it important for Christians to give serious thought to our mortality? Stated another way, what is the importance of our observance of Ash Wednesday? Or stating it yet another way, how do thoughts about death assist us in living well? Perhaps these thoughts of Kathleen Norris could help in considering this matter:

"When I first read the Rule of St. Benedict many years ago, his injunction 'to keep death daily before your eyes' seemed morbid, epitomizing a negative stereotype of the stern, ascetic monk. But having spent the better part of five years helping to provide first my father, and then my husband, with a good death, I find that Benedict's words now console and guide me. They call me to be more merciful in my dealings with other mortals and with myself."[82]

4. Are there things other than those mentioned in this poem that need to be said about this topic?

Scriptures for further reflection:

Genesis 3:19
Job 19:25-26
Psalm 49:16-17
Ecclesiastes 3:1-2 3:20, and 12:7
John 3:16
I Corinthians 15:42-58
Revelation 21:1-4

THE COLLAR

I struck the board, and cried, No more.
           I will abroad.
     What? Shall I ever sigh and pine?
My lines and life are free; free as the road,
        Loose as the wind, as large as store.   5
           Shall I be still in suit?
Have I no harvest but a thorn
To let me blood, and not restore
What I have lost with cordial fruit?
             Sure there was wine   10
Before my sighs did dry it: there was corn
         Before my tears did drown it.
    Is the year only lost to me?
         Have I no bays to crown it?
No flowers, no garlands gay? all blasted?   15
         All wasted?
Not so, my heart: but there is fruit,
         And thou hast hands.
     Recover all thy sigh-blown age
On double pleasures: leave thy cold dispute   20
Of what is fit, and not. Forsake thy cage,
         Thy rope of sands,
Which petty thoughts have made, and made to thee
     Good cable, to enforce and draw,
         And be thy law,   25
    While thou didst wink and wouldst not see.
        Away; take heed:
        I will abroad.
Call in thy death's head there: tie up thy fears.
        He that forbears   30
     To suit and serve his need,
        Deserves his load.
But as I raved and grew more fierce and wild
        At every word,
Me thoughts I heard one calling, *Child!*   35
       And I replied, *My Lord.*

The Big Picture

"The poem is dramatizing a state of mind..."[83]

This poem reflects the inner turmoil of the speaker and has several voices. The first voice is an angry complaint from the heart of the speaker (lines 1-16), then a reasoned reply by the will (lines 17-26), followed by an intense response by the heart (lines 27-32); finally two voices conclude the poem (lines 33-36). The poem is driven by the intensity of conflict, but finds its resolution in the devotion and tenderness of submission.

The Parts of the Picture

The Title. There have been numerous speculations about the meaning of the title. The term "collar" was used to indicate discipline and restraint associated with conscience (with the accompanying expression "to slip the collar"). Hence, the title could indicate the struggle with restraint found within the poem. The title also could refer to a slave's collar. It could also be a play on the word "choler" meaning "anger." Or as a pun on "caller," the title could refer to the call of the sinner to righteousness in Luke 5:32, or to the call to take on the yoke of Christ in Matthew 11:29-30, or to the One calling the speaker in the penultimate line of the poem. The richness of the poem accommodates all these meanings, some perhaps better than others.[84]

Lines 1-16. The tone of this first section is captured in the decision declared in the first two lines: "I struck the board, and cried, No more/ I will abroad." Thus the poem opens abruptly with the rebellious anger of the striking of the communion board (the altar) and the determined finality of the statement of fleeing "abroad" (away or out of doors or in different directions). Lines 3-5 declare independence. The speaker will not "sigh and pine" since the "lines" or directions for his life (or perhaps, also, the lines of his verse)[85] are akin to the freedom of the road, the looseness of the wind, and the quantity of abundance. Lines 6-9 intensify this mood with questions: Shall the speaker continue "still" (yet or silent or unrewarded) in his "suit" or petition? Will his only harvest be a thorn causing him to bleed rather than restoring the loss of "cordial" or healing fruit? The harvest imagery continues in lines 10-12 with the concession that once there was wine and corn (allusions to the wine and bread of the Eucharist and a connection to the striking and leaving the communion board in line 1), but these have been lost in his sighs that dry the wine and tears that drown the corn. Questions reappear in rapid-fire fashion with increasing bitterness in lines 13-16 along with more images of failed fruition. Is only the year lost? (Or is it only lost to him? Or both?) Are there not any bay leaves (symbols of triumph) to crown the year? And are not all the flowers and garlands "blasted," "wasted"?

Lines 17-26. The beginning of "Not so, my heart" marks a significant change in the voice and tone of the poem. The voice that now speaks is a carefully reasoned one. This is not a change in the person of the speaker but a change to another part of the same speaker as the inner turmoil of speaker continues to be revealed. This reasoned voice points out that there is a way out of the heart's anger. The heart is not helpless. There is fruit, and the heart has hands with which to grasp it. The way out is found in the three imperatives in lines 19-26. First, the heart is to recover "on" (or by means of) "double pleasures" the age blown away by the heart's sighs. This recovery can be accomplished by leaving the "cold dispute" about what is fit and not. The heart is to forsake the "cage, / Thy rope of sands" made by "petty thoughts." This "rope of sands" (or fruitless activity)[86] has been made into "Good cable" and used by the heart to "enforce and draw, / And be thy law" while the heart failed to see what was happening.

Lines 27-32. The argument of reason in the preceding lines is now abruptly rebutted by the heart with "Away; take heed" followed by a restatement of the decision that began the poem: "I will abroad." In short, the heart is unmoved by reason's argument in lines 17-26. Reason is to heed this. Furthermore, reason is admonished to "call in thy death's head" (perhaps this is the force of reason that leads toward death) and to "tie up" or stop using fears. The heart's final word (a word consistent with the self-centeredness of the heart throughout) reminds reason that whoever fails to take care of himself first or "suit and serve his need" deserves the load he carries. The heart's rejection of reason is thereby finalized.

Lines 33-36. In a resolution of greatly conflicting forces, the poem concludes with a sudden and radical reversal. As the speaker "rav'd and grew more fierce and wild/ At every word," there comes an inner sense of a calling to the speaker as "Child." The reply of the speaker reveals the resolution of his inner turmoil, a resolution found in the commitment, the submission, the devotion of "My Lord."

The Parts of the Picture Come Together

The path of this poem follows the voices. Because of the clashing of these voices, the poem is one of disharmony. As pointed out by Joseph Summers, "The object of imitation is the disordered life of self-will which rebels against the will of God and therefore lacks the order and harmony of art as well as of the religious life."[87]

The voice of the speaker's heart clearly establishes the tone of violence ("I struck"), of emotion ("I cried"), and of leave taking ("I will abroad."). A series of questions wrought with bitterness heightens the intensity as the heart justifies its decision to leave. Shall the heart always "sigh and pine"? Shall it always be the suitor? Is its only harvest a thorn? Its harvest has come to naught: no longer is there any invigorating fruit, the wine is dried up, the corn drown, there are no bays leaves of triumph, and flowers and garland are blasted, wasted. The voice is almost hysterical, one of harsh rebellion. Chaos has come— the chaos of passionate self-pity.

Then another voice speaks. This one attempts to right the course, to restore order, to restrain the raging. No questions come from this voice; instead, blunt disagreement and the firm statement of an alternative view emerge. This voice points out that there is fruit, and the heart has hands to grasp it. Take action, this voice counsels, in a certain way: recover pleasure, release the dispute, and forsake the cage foolishly and blindly constructed by petty thoughts. This advice strikes directly in a tightly reasoned fashion. Surely this is enough to stem the tide of rage momentarily—if the heart will consent.

But the heart will not consent. The voice of the heart returns to its initial declaration: "I will abroad." A restatement of his self-centered pathos follows: he that fails to serve his own need deserves the load that falls upon him.

As the turmoil of debate within the speaker heightens, he grows "more fierce and wild/ At every word." Then another voice calls, or so the speaker thinks. Whatever doubt, if any, is raised by the "Me thoughts" quickly disappears in the clarity and simplicity of this voice's calling: "Child." This call is for relationship, a certain kind of relationship, the kind of relationship that is right for the Kingdom of God (see Mark 10:13-15). This call is beyond anger and reason. This call to relationship elicits an immediate response of relationship consummated: "My Lord."

In this climax is a brilliant touch of irony. Throughout its raging rebellion, the speaker's heart has characterized itself as a slave with nothing to show for its efforts. This slave is so bitter that he strikes the altar and all associated with it as he decides to leave. The heart is also angered by the voice of reason's attempt to reassess the facts and point out another course of action. But this heart, so overwrought by the altar and so further angered by the voice of reason, immediately responds to the intimacy of the call of relationship from the One who views the speaker as Child. This kind of relationship goes beyond the fierce and wild anger of the heart, beyond reason's calculated advice. This call to relationship is based on the intimate love of parent and child. To this call the speaker (like Thomas in John 20:28) can respond "My Lord" and thereby consummate the relationship with praise, worship, and submission. The defiant rebel who felt like a scorned slave has found his place and his peace as a Child rightly related to his Lord.

Reflections

1. What does this poem have to say about relationship with God?
2. What spiritual direction does it provide?
3. Have you experienced a similar sense of spiritual disorder like that manifested in this poem, a sense of rebellion wanting to break loose along with a sense of reason contesting this rebellion? If so, how did you respond?
4. If someone asked you how to respond to this kind of situation, what would you say? Is this poem helpful in formulating an answer?
5. How do you respond to the resolution found in the last two lines of the poem? Is your understanding of this resolution based—
    a. on reason alone,
    b. on emotion,
    c. on your own experience that includes both reason and emotion, or
    d. on something else?

Scriptures for further reflection:

Psalm 13
Matthew 18:1-4
John 20:16 and 24-29
Philippians 3:4-9

LIFE

I made a posy, while the day ran by:
Here will I smell my remnant out, and tie
                    My life within this band.
But Time did beckon to the flowers, and they
By noon most cunningly did steal away,   5
                    And withered in my hand.

My hand was next to them, and then my heart:
I took, without more thinking, in good part
                    Time's gentle admonition:
Who did so sweetly death's sad taste convey,   10
Making my mind to smell my fatal day;
                    Yet sugaring the suspicion.

Farewell dear flowers, sweetly your time you spent,
Fit, while you lived, for smell or ornament,
                    And after death for cures.   15
I follow straight without complaints or grief,
Since if my scent be good, I care not if
It be as short as yours.

The Big Picture

How are we to live our lives in light of the brevity of life? In this poem, Herbert deals with this subject by observing a bouquet of flowers. As the speaker describes his making a bouquet of flowers one day only to see them wither by noon of that same day, he reflects on how he desires to live his life just as did the flowers.

The Parts of the Picture

Stanza 1. Here is the making and withering of the "posy" or Bouquet of flowers ("posy" can also mean a poem). From this description the speaker draws the lessons of the poem. The first three lines portray the making of the bouquet, the pleasure of the speaker's smelling the remnants of the cut flowers, and of his "tying" (or somehow intertwining or investing) his life "within this band." Lines 4-6 introduce time and its effects. By noon, "time did beckon to the flowers," and, while he holds them, they wither.

Stanza 2. What is to be learned from the experience portrayed in stanza 1? Line 7 gives a brief but poignant portrait of the poet's intimate identity, both in "hand" and "heart," with the flowers. In his experience with the flowers, he perceives "Time's gentle admonition." The admonition conveys "so sweetly death's sad taste," and his "mind smells" (something unexpected of the mind) his "fatal day," sugar coated though it be.

Stanza 3. How does one respond to the lesson of life's brevity portrayed in stanza 2? The first three lines of stanza 3 are directed to the flowers as he bids them adieu and praises how well they lived ("for smell or ornament") and how useful they are even in death. The reference "for cures" in line 15 is an allusion to the medicinal use of roses in Herbert's time.[88] In the concluding three lines, the speaker makes clear his response to the example of the flowers: without complaint he will follow them and devote himself to living well (or to making his "scent be good" as the flowers did) without regard to how brief that living may be.

The Parts of the Picture Come Together

First there is the coming together of the speaker and the bouquet of flowers. Not only is there the making of the bouquet, there is also the tying of the speaker's "life within this band." Then time's invasive beckoning of the flowers causes them to "steal away." The tie between bouquet and speaker, however, is not broken. It is out of this tying together of speaker and flowers, and out of their staying together despite the flowers' withering and stealing away, that the lessons about "life" emerge.

Because of the staying together of the speaker and flowers, the poem is primarily about "life" and not death (even though time and death play prominent roles in the learning of the lessons of life). Despite the gentle admonition of time and the taste of death, what emerges continues to be tied to, and rooted in, the flowers, even as they are bid farewell. As the flowers have made good use of their brief time, so too the speaker resolves to do the same with his own brief time. Even as the flowers leave, the speaker follows them "straight," maintaining the tie of speaker and flowers. The flowers die, the speaker lives, but the tie remains, as living well triumphs over living only briefly. That is the flow of the poem. As the tie of the speaker and the flowers continues, so does the flow, the driving force, of the poem.

Herbert frequently finds life in death. Often he speaks of ties that cannot be broken by death. That kind of comment by him is usually made within the context of eternal life. In this poem, however, Herbert speaks of life triumphant over death within the context of the here and now. In the example of life well lived by some flowers, Herbert finds the goodness and victory of life lived well on this earth. Speaker and flowers are tied together and remain together in abundant, albeit brief, life.

Reflections

1. The poem does not mention God. Does it, however, indirectly speak to the issue of relationship with God?
2. What spiritual direction does it provide?
3. The speaker of the poem found a valuable lesson about living from the life and death of some flowers and from the experience of investing himself in those flowers. Who are the people and/or what are the other things in which you have invested your life and from which you have learned valuable lessons about living?
4. In what ways does a healthy meditation about the brevity of life on this earth help us to live well?

Scriptures for further reflection:

Psalm 39:4
Psalm 90:5-6; 12
Psalm 103:15-18
John 10:10

JUSTICE (I)

I cannot skill of these thy ways.
Lord, thou didst make me, yet thou woundest me;
Lord, thou dost wound me, yet thou dost relieve me:
Lord, thou relievest, yet I die by thee:
Lord, thou dost kill me, yet thou dost reprieve me.   5

But when I mark my life and praise,
Thy justice me most fitly pays:
For, I do praise thee, yet I praise thee not:
My prayers mean thee, yet my prayers stray:
I would do well, yet sin the hand hath got: 10
My soul doth love thee, yet it loves delay.
I cannot skill of these my ways.

The Big Picture

This poem is about lack of understanding. First, the speaker states his lack of understanding of God's ways with him. Then the speaker realizes that he has an even greater lack of understanding about his own ways with God. This is confession—done in an unusual manner. What starts out as a frustrating attempt to understand God's ways ends up being a realization that the speaker's own ways are more confusing than God's. It's an unusual way (and potentially a productive way) of approaching the issue of understanding God's ways.

The Parts of the Picture

The first five lines are focused on God's confusing ways, the second seven lines are on the speaker's confusing ways. After the declaration "I cannot skill [understand] of these thy ways," the Lord is addressed four times with each address declaring a contradiction in God's actions. With "But" in line 6, however, the poem takes a turn that changes its whole nature. The issue is now the "marking" or identifying or examining the speaker's life and how he praises. When the speaker looks at himself, he can "most fitly pay" or respect God's justice, for the speaker's failures (in his praise, prayers, actions, and love) are graphic. The poem ends as it began—with a lack of understanding, but this time, the confusion, with subtle humor, derives from trying to understand the speaker's own ways.

The Parts of the Picture Come Together

Initially everything in the poem points to the failure of God's justice or at least to the confusing nature of His ways with the speaker. Evidence is provided of this injustice as examples are systematically presented in the first stanza of the apparent injustice of God. Surely the poem is headed in the direction of a complaint or personal lament. Surely the next step will be for the speaker to call on God to justify His ways. But the poem takes a dramatic turn. A lament becomes a confession.

The speaker realizes that dealing with the issue of justice begins with his own actions and failures. Compared to the failures in the speaker's life, the justice of God fares well. The poem, then, brings the speaker to confession rather than criticism. It is a poem of jarring reversal that refocuses and redirects the inquiry of justice. It is a poem that engenders expectations of evaluating God's ways but then suddenly sweeps in the opposite direction to self-evaluation. In doing so, it provides helpful perspective on an important dimension of relationship with God without attempting to justify the ways of God to man or resolve the mystery of God's ways.

Reflections

1. What does the poem have to say about relationship with God?
2. What spiritual direction does it provide?
3. How do you respond to the poem's implication that an inquiry about the justice of God's ways should begin with an inquiry into one's own ways?
   Do you agree? Disagree? Both?
4. Is confession the starting point in every aspect of our relationship with God? Why? Why not?

Scriptures for further reflection:

Isaiah 55:8-9
Ezekial 18:29-30
Romans 7:15-20
Galatians 5:17

THE PULLEY

When God at first made man,
Having a glass of blessings standing by;
Let us (said he) pour on him all we can:
Let the world's riches, which dispersed lie,
    Contract into a span.   5

So strength first made a way;
Then beauty flowed, then wisdom, honour, pleasure:
When almost all was out, God made a stay,
Perceiving that alone of all his treasure
    Rest in the bottom lay.   10

For if I should (said he)
Bestow this jewel also on my creature,
He would adore my gifts instead of me,
And rest in Nature, not the God of Nature:
    So both should losers be.   15

Yet let him keep the rest,
But keep them with repining restlessness:
Let him be rich and weary, that at least,
If goodness lead him not, yet weariness
    May toss him to my breast.   20

The Big Picture

"You made us for yourself and our hearts find no peace until they rest in you."[89] These words of Augustine state well the theme of this poem. It is a poem, as Helen Vendler describes it, with an "edge or frame of frivolity or entertainment about the whole."[90] As Vendler also points out, the poem "creates a myth to answer a riddle."[91] The myth concerns the story of creation and the riddle asks the question of "Why is mankind so rich in blessings and yet so restless?" The answer to the riddle unfolds in the telling of the story.

The Parts of the Picture

Stanzas 1- 2. Lines 1-5 contain this poem's story of creation of man. It is portrayed as God's pouring the blessings of the world's riches upon man. In lines 6-10, the details of the blessings are given. But then God paused (or "made a stay") and considered the blessing that remained—"rest." Should it be bestowed upon man, also?

Stanza 3. The problem is that if "rest" is given, mankind would adore the gifts and not the Giver. Mankind would, in short, "rest" (note the connection of lines 10, 14, and 16 by the play on this word) "in Nature, not the God of Nature," thereby disrupting the whole purpose of creation for both God and man.

Stanza 4. The "Yet" beginning of this stanza prepares us for the resolution to the problem posed in stanza 3. Man will keep all the other blessings but will do without "rest." And there is a reason for this. Without "rest," man's weariness will "toss" man to God's "breast" (even when "goodness" fails to do so), thereby restoring the intended relationship of God and man.

The Parts of the Picture Come Together

The poem possesses the elements and charm of good storytelling. There is the beginning with God's announcement of the intention of creation. In the middle, this intention is carried out successfully until a problem arises. The resolution to this problem comes in the ending as the original intention of creation is preserved in the image of mankind finding its rest in God's breast.

In the telling of the story emerge insights into the nature of both the creature and the Creator. God's desire for the best for mankind comes early on. God's understanding of his creature is presented next. If given everything, this creature will become god-like, admiring self and not God. God's wisdom is revealed in the resolution of the problem. Finally, man's restlessness is understood, ironically, as a blessing that is connected to God's desire for intimate relationship with His creature. And all of this attests to the truth proclaimed by the prophet Isaiah that the ways of God are not the ways of man. (Isaiah 55:8-9).

Reflections

1. What does this poem have to say about relationship with God?
2. What spiritual direction does it provide?
3. How do you respond to the poem? How true is it for you?
4. What are the things that bring you back to the "breast" of God?

Scriptures for further reflection:

Psalm 62:1-2; 5-8
Psalm 91:1-6
Matthew 11:28-30

THE DISCHARGE

Busy enquiring heart, what wouldst thou know?
Why dost thou pry,
And turn, and leer, and with a licorous eye
Look high and low;
And in thy lookings stretch and grow?   5

Hast thou not made thy counts, and summed up all?
Did not thy heart
Give up the whole, and with the whole depart?
Let what will fall:
That which is past who can recall?   10

Thy life is God's, thy time to come is gone,
And is his right.
He is thy night at noon: he is at night
Thy noon alone.
The crop is his, for he hath sown.   15

And well it was for thee, when this befell,
That God did make
Thy business his, and in thy life partake:
For thou canst tell,
If it be his once, all is well.   20

Only the present is thy part and fee.
And happy thou,
If, though thou didst not beat thy future brow,
Thou couldst well see
What present things required of thee.   25

They ask enough; why shouldst thou further go?
Raise not the mud
Of future depths, but drink the clear and good.
Dig not for woe
In times to come; for it will grow.   30

Man and the present fit: if he provide,
                    He breaks the square.
This hour is mine: if for the next I care,
                    I grow too wide,
            And do encroach upon death's side.   35

For death each hour environs and surrounds.
                    He that would know
And care for future chances, cannot go
                    Unto those grounds,
            But through a Church-yard which them bounds.   40

Things present shrink and die: but they that spend
                    Their thoughts and sense
On future grief, do not remove it thence,
                    But it extend,
            And draw the bottom out an end.   45

God chains the dog till night: wilt loose the chain,
                    And wake thy sorrow?
Wilt thou forestall it, and now grieve tomorrow,
                    And then again
            Grieve over freshly all thy pain?   50

Either grief will not come: or if it must,
                    Do not forecast.
And while it cometh, it is almost past.
                    Away distrust:
            My God hath promised; he is just.   55

The Big Picture

This poem reflects the tension of the speaker as he tries to guide his "busy inquiring heart" toward the peace found by trusting God in the present moment. Ultimately peace is to be found in the realization that "Thy life is God's" (line 11). Along the way, the speaker tries to discharge from his heart those anxieties about the past and future that work against this peace. (See Luke 12:22-40 and Matthew 6:25-34).

The Parts of the Picture

Stanza 1. The questions here focus on the "busy inquiring" nature of the speaker's heart. The restlessness of his heart is portrayed in terms of: seeking knowledge ("inquiring" and "know"); intruding ("pry"); looking ("leer and with a lickerous eye [one with a sharp desire for pleasure]/ Look high and low"); and stretching and growing.

Stanza 2. More questions—this time they concern the heart's dealing with the past. Has the heart not squared past accounts and let go of them? Who can even recall the past since it is the past?

Stanzas 3-4. Here is the core concept of the poem: "Thy life is God's." Questions disappear as statements emerge. The statements flow out of this core concept. Because life is God's, all is His: the "time to come," the night and noontime, and "the crop" or produce of the speaker's life. And it is well that God partakes and possesses the speaker's life.

Stanzas 5 through 7. The focus shifts from God to the present moment. It is in the present that God desires the speaker and his heart to live. There the heart can find happiness. The "present things" ask enough; hence there is no need to "Raise ... the muddle of future depths" or "Dig ... for woe/In times to come." Since man and the present moment "fit," providing or planning for the future "breaks the square" or "the fit." In caring for the future rather than the present moment, the speaker grows "too wide" and encroaches on the realm of death.

Stanza 8. Having introduced the subject of death, the speaker uses it here as another illustration of the futility of focusing on the future. Even though death surrounds each hour, the only way to death is through the graveyard, not through caring "for future chances."

Stanzas 9-10. More reasons are given for not focusing on the grief, affliction, and sorrow that the future will bring. Rather than removing future grief, concern over this grief extends it. The effect of this concern over the future is like reaching the end of a skein of thread (line 45) or, said another way, coming up short of material to work with. Questions (as in stanzas 1 and 2) return in stanza 10. God has chained the dog of sorrow until night comes; does the heart desire to awake that sorrow prematurely? Or, in a similar vein, will the heart today grieve tomorrow's sorrow and thereby double the pain by grieving it again tomorrow?

Stanza 11. The ending is matter-of-fact and triumphant. Grief will either come or not, but in any case, there is no need to forecast it. Rather than doing that, there is a better way: discharge distrust and trust the promises of God who is just.

The Parts of the Picture Come Together

F.E. Hutchinson points out that "the word discharge is used for a document conveying release from an obligation...."[93] This is a good starting point for considering the movement of thought within the poem. It is, after all, a poem about discharging. That which is to be discharged is the senseless concern about the past and future, a concern that prevents the speaker from realizing the fullness of the present moment. This discharge begins with stern, direct questioning of the speaker's restless heart. The questions bring to light the anxiety there– the prying, the turning, the leering of its "lookings." Why is all this going on? Has the heart not settled and let go of past accounts?

Then the questions cease as the speaker directly asserts the answer to the heart's troubling condition. And with this, the poem turns to God. The answers come clearly, briskly: your life is God's; God has made you His business; all is well; live in the fullness of the present moment since "man and the present fit."

Enough said—or so it seems. The answer is stated—but the restlessness remains. The focus turns to the future. What about death? And other future sorrows? More answers come. Death surrounds all, but can be dealt with only in the graveyard. And the sorrows of the future are made only worse by anticipating them in the present. Then, having moved through past, present, and future, the speaker concludes with the bottom line: trust God.

This is a poem that rides with the tension of the speaker's inner struggle. Beginning with the prying, turning, and leering of the speaker's heart, the poem "discharges" the sources of this anxiety. In fact, these sources are really one—a fruitless wandering away from living in the present. And if the problem is singular, so is the resolution: trusting God while living in the present moment.

It is a poem that thrusts the problem forth (stanzas 1 and 2) and then presents the resolution early on (stanzas 3 and 4). It then weaves together the problem and the resolution over the remaining stanzas. In this interweaving, the discharging takes place as the problem is presented several times, and the resolution is stated and restated. It is a way of problem solving in which the resolution is clear and certain. This is not Herbert's usual way. Often there is more ambiguity, more struggle, more seeing through a glass darkly, and finally a resolution. But here there is clarity and certainty. Perhaps this is simply an important aspect of Herbert re-emerging. Although the struggle and ambiguity were prominent in his inner struggles with self and God, there was an abiding resolution to which he often returned. That resolution is clear and certain in this poem: your life is God's. Living with this resolution is the key to discharging needless anxiety about the past and future and living in the present moment.

Reflections

1. What does this poem have to say about relationship with God?
2. What spiritual direction does it provide?
3. The poem deals with various causes of anxiety that need "discharging"? How would you define the causes of your anxieties? Is the poem helpful in defining these causes?
4. The poem also deals with the "discharge" of causes of anxiety? How do you "discharge" your anxieties? Is the poem helpful in this regard?

Scriptures for further reflection:
Matthew 6:25-34
Philippians 4:6-7
1 Timothy 6:6-8
Hebrews 13:5-6
1 Peter 5:6-7

SION

Lord, with what glory wast thou served of old,
When Solomon's temple stood and flourished!
      Where most things were of purest gold;
      The wood was all embellished
With flowers and carvings, mystical and rare: 5
All showed the builders, craved the seer's care.

Yet all this glory, all this pomp and state
Did not affect thee much, was not thy aim;
      Something there was, that sowed debate:
      Wherefore thou quittest thy ancient claim: 10
And now thy Architecture meets with sin;
For all thy frame and fabric is within.

There thou art struggling with a peevish heart,
Which sometimes crosseth thee, thou sometimes it:
      The fight is hard on either part.   15
      Great God doth fight, he doth submit.
All Solomon's sea of brass and world of stone
Is not so dear to thee as one good groan.

And truly brass and stones are heavy things,
Tombs for the dead, not temples fit for thee: 20
      But groans are quick, and full of wings,
      And all their motions upward be;
And ever as they mount, like larks they sing;
The note is sad, yet music for a King.

The Big Picture

Where does God dwell? What is He doing? And what is the outcome of His efforts? This poem deals with each of these issues as it makes its case for God's presence in the human heart. It begins with a description of the extravagance of Solomon's temple and then tells of God's choice to reject that temple and reside instead in the human heart. There a struggle ensues as God battles sin. But all is well as out of the struggle emerges "one good groan," a sad note indeed but also the sign of the contrition of a sinner, and as such, it soars on wings as music to God the King.

The Parts of the Picture

Title. Sion is a variant spelling of "Zion," the mountain and location of the city of David and Solomon's temple. It is a place associated with the presence of God (see descriptions of Solomon's temple in I Kings 6 and II Chronicles 3-4).

Stanza 1. The glory of the gold, the embellished wood, and the rare decorations of Solomon's temple are described, all revealing the care of the builders and the cravings of those who see it.

Stanza 2. A new element is introduced—the contrast of Solomon's temple and the new dwelling place of God. All of the glory of Solomon's temple failed to interest God. The cause of this "debate" is mysteriously hidden in the phrase "Something there was" (line 9) that caused God to "quit" the "ancient claim" upon Him by the temple. Lines 11 and 12 inform of the new dwelling place of the "frame and fabric" of God as it "meets with sin" within man. In man God now dwells (see I Corinthians 3:16) and therein "meets with sin."

Stanza 3. Lines 13-16 portray the struggle between God and man's "peevish" (discontented or ill-tempered) heart. Amazingly, God chooses to "submit" to this hard fight. Lines 17 and 18 introduce a new topic that is related to the fight but also begin a transition to the triumphant conclusion of the next stanza. This is the "one good groan" that is dearer to God than all of Solomon's brass and stone. The reason for this becomes clear in the next stanza.

Stanza 4. The contrast between the outer and inner temple, so evident in stanzas 1 and 2, returns in this stanza. Lines 19 and 20 make clear that a temple of brass and stones is unsuitable for the Lord—they are merely "Tombs for the dead." In contrast, "groans are quick" or full of life, of wings, of motion, of song. These groans are like the "one good groan" introduced in line 18, groans that emerge from the struggle between God and sin in man's "peevish heart." Because they are an act of contrition by a sinner, their "note is sad," but, for the same reason, they are music to God.

The Parts of the Picture Come Together

The first element of the poem is neutral. It does not take sides; instead, it describes. In fact, in this beginning, there are no sides to take, only a rendering of the glory that was Solomon's temple. Then the poem takes an abrupt turn. There is rejection. Such a temple with all its gold and wood and decorations, such a monument to its builder's care, so impressive to those who saw it—"Yet all this glory" missed God's aim. There is, therefore, a "quitting," a letting go by God of this wondrous place to dwell. God chooses instead to reside within His own creature, mankind. This choice comes with a high cost, the cost of the struggle with sin. Simply put, "The fight is hard." (line 15) And, amazingly, God submits to this struggle.

As the struggle with sin becomes dominant in stanza 3, "the whole pace of the poem changes," as Richard Strier points out: "Instead of the rather stately mock meditative tone of stanza 1, and the rather dry, explanatory tone of lines 7-10, the tone is now excited and dramatic." The portrayal of God changes, also. "God is suddenly not the object of worship but an intimate contender."

But why has God made this choice to reject Solomon's temple and dwell within the heart of man and struggle there with sin? The answer comes in the poem's final movement. The struggle is worth the effort because of "one good groan" (line 18). Groans are the opposite of the brass and stones of a temple. The heavy things of brass and stone are tombs. In contrast, "Groans are quick," full of life, a product of authentic and spontaneous contrition by the sinner. They mount upward, "full of wings," and although contrition makes their note a sad one, it also makes them into music to God for they are a sign that sin has been confessed and thereby overcome.

The poem, therefore, moves from the glory of Solomon's temple through God's rejection of that temple with His choice to reside in man's peevish heart and then concludes on the lively note of a groan of contrition signifying victory over sin. But there is also another way in which the parts of the poem come together. The poem is driven by contrasts. First, there is the contrast of the outward temple built by Solomon and the inward temple of man's heart. In addition there is the contrast in the arrangement of the parts of the poem. Initially portrayed is the glory of Solomon's temple followed by God's rejection of that temple as a dwelling place. Then there is the intensity of the struggle against sin in the heart of man resolved by the music of the lively, soaring sad note of a groan. From the portrayal of glory to the rejection of that glory, from the fierceness of battle to its resolution with a groan, the poem twice pulls one way and then another. It is contrast that somewhat surprises but does so with a force that gives energy to its portrayal of God's nature, dwelling place, and victory.

Above all else, this is a poem about God. What emerges out of these movements within the poem is an intimate, involved combative, compassionate, victorious God who rejects the glory of brass and stone and the appeal of gold and embellished wood and chooses to dwell in the heart of man and do battle with sin. This, of course, is the God revealed in Jesus Christ, the One who battled sin on mankind's behalf so that the sad but repentant note of the sinner's groan may become pleasing to God's ear.

Reflections

1. What does this poem have to say about relationship with God?
2. What spiritual direction does it offer?
3. Is the working of God within you similar to or different from (or both) the working of God as reflected in this poem? How do you know of the nature of His working within you?
4. Although the poem is clearly about the nature of God and His workings, there is obviously a human component in all this. How would you describe the struggle of God and sin within yourself? What are the forces that drive that struggle? What are ways in which the struggle is resolved (if it is)? What part do you play in the resolution of the struggle?

Scriptures for further reflection:

John 14:15-17
I Corinthians 6:19
II Corinthians 1:21-22
Galatians 5:16-26

THE CHURCH FLOOR

Mark you the floor? That square and speckled stone,
　　Which looks so firm and strong,
　　　　Is *Patience*:

And the other black and grave, wherewith each one
　　Is checkered all along,　　　　　　　　　　5
　　　　Humility:

The gentle rising, which on either hand
　　Leads to the choir above,
　　　　Is *Confidence*:

But the sweet cement, which in one sure band　　10
　　Ties the whole frame, is Love
　　　　And *Charity*.

　　Hither sometimes Sin steals, and stains
　　The marble's neat and curious veins:
But all is cleansed when the marble weeps.　　15
　　Sometimes Death, puffing at the door,
　　Blows all the dust about the floor:
But while he thinks to spoil the room, he sweeps.
　　Blest be the *Architect*, whose art
　　Could build so strong in a weak heart.　　20

The Big Picture

What's in a church floor? Plenty, says this poem. This is another of Herbert's poems that uses a physical aspect of the church to make a statement about God's work (see also *The Windows* and *Church Monuments*). In short, the poem reveals the elements and work of the church floor and then makes an imaginative connection with a spiritual truth. Until the final two lines, the poem focuses on two things: (1) the elements of the floor (patience, humility, confidence, and love), and (2) the work of the floor (combating sin and death). Then, the poet goes beyond the church floor to the human heart. As the church floor has been constructed with the proper elements to carry out its work, so also God has constructed the human heart to carry out its work.

The Parts of the Picture

The first four stanzas (lines 1-12) are separated by a space between each of them. Each stanza is devoted to a virtue ("firm and strong" patience; humility with which each stone is "checkered"; "gentle rising" confidence; and the "sweet cement" of charity). Each virtue is a piece of the floor

Lines 13-18. The church floor (now one unit instead of separate parts) is able to confront sin and death. Sin "stains" the floor, but when the floor "weeps" or sweats "all is cleansed." And Death, "puffing at the doore" blows dust all about, but ironically, in doing so, it cleans the floor by sweeping it or by having someone sweep the dust.

Lines 19-20. It is to God the Architect that the final couplet is offered in praise: "Blest be the Architect" who is able to "build so strong in a weak heart."

The Parts of the Picture Come Together

The poem begins with an imperative: "Mark you." With this the reader's attention is called to elements of the church floor. Four elements are considered: *Patience* ("firm and strong"); *Humility* ("black and grave"); *Confidence* ("the gentle rising"): and *Love* ("the sweet cement"). The parts are thereby presented.

The poem now makes another movement, or put another way, it takes a different shape. The shape of lines 13-20 changes as does the focus of the poem. As Coburn Freer points out, "the stanza shape determines the argument of the poem."[95] Now no space separates stanzas. The lines reflect a whole as if the parts of the floor are now united. And although separate thoughts are still expressed in three-line structures in lines 13-18 (as they are in lines 1-12), the third line in each of these structures is the longest line rather than the shortest. Each of these third lines (lines 15 and 18) begins with "But" and is used by the poet to invert the thought of the previous two lines rather than completing the thought of those lines (as do the last line of the first four stanzas).

As the shape of the lines is changed, so is the content. The focus is now on the work of the floor as it confronts sin and death. Sin stains the floor but "all is cleansed when the marble weeps." In short, the marble is able to sweat or "weep" to cleanse itself of sin. The analogy of the cleansing effect of the marble's "weeping" to the weeping of confession and the cleansing of sin is apparent, as pointed out by Richard Strier: "By referring to a ... property of marble [i.e., its ability to "sweat" or "weep"], Herbert restores our sense that he is really talking about marble as well as about penitence here, that he is still exploring analogies between spiritual and physical phenomena."[96]

The first of the abilities of the church floor, therefore, is to thwart sin. The second ability of the floor is to reverse the workings of death. Again the work of the adversary is stated first: death "puffing at the door" blows dust "about the floor." The effects of the adversary are then nullified, this time with a bit of irony as the puffing that was meant to dirty the floor ends up sweeping it (or having it swept). To be sure, the dust slights the appearance of the floor—but only briefly, and it really does nothing to permeate, or in any way significantly damage, it.

The poem seems to have accomplished its purpose. The power of the foundation of the church (with its elements of patience, humility, confidence, and love) defeats the effects of sin and death. But the poet is not finished. In the concluding couplet, the poem takes the reader beyond the church floor. In characteristic Herbert fashion, we are provided with a surprise ending. As Strier says, "We have been caught off guard."[97] The primary focus of the poem shifts dramatically. It is now on the Architect and the human heart. The first 18 lines have served as a means to a greater end. As important as the church floor is, the greater lesson concerns God and the human heart.

The poem that began by instructing the reader ends with praise of God. Like He did with the floor, God can take patience, humility, confidence, and love and transform the weak human heart into something as strong as the floor, something that can overcome sin and death. As Strier so aptly states:

"What we are left contemplating is ... the unique ability of God to create imperishable virtues [such as patience, humility, confidence, and love] in the human heart—virtues which enable the regenerate to achieve true penitence and escape fear of death... The point of the poem is ... to focus our attention on where the poet's is focused—on the work of God in the individual Christian's heart ... The poem ends when it reveals the individual heart as the center of Christianity."[98]

Reflections

1. What does the poem have to say about relationship with God?
2. What spiritual direction does it provide?
3. As indicated by the speaker's beginning imperative address to the reader ("Mark you"), he intends to instruct. For what purpose? To educate? To convict? To encourage? To praise? To delight? Or all of these and more?
4. In what way(s), if any, is the poem helpful to you? If you find it convicting or encouraging, in what way(s)?
5. In addition to patience, humility, confidence, and love, are there other virtues that you consider essential to the heart of a Christian?
6. One could possibly argue that in this poem Herbert states a "works theology" in that he emphasizes human characteristics (such as patience, humility, confidence, and charity), rather than the blood of Christ, as the elements for defeating sin and death. Do you agree with such an argument? Why or why not?

Scriptures for further reflection:

I Samuel 16:7
Proverbs 4:23
Isaiah 45:9-10
Jeremiah 18:1-6
Isaiah 64:8
Matthew 5:8
I Peter 2:4-5

THE QUIDDITY

My God, a verse is not a crown,
No point of honor, or gay suit,
No hawk, or banquet, or renown,
Nor a good sword, nor yet a lute:

It cannot vault, or dance, or play;   5
It never was in France or Spain;
Nor can it entertain the day
With my great stable or demesne:

It is no office, art, or news,
Nor the Exchange, or busy Hall;   10
But it is that which while I use
I am with thee, and most take all.

The Big Picture

What did George Herbert think of poetry? This poem deals with that question as the poet speaks to God about what poetry is not and then declares, in the final two lines, the essence of poetry to him. This is an offering to God, a poem directed to God, a poem in which poetry itself is identified with the poet's experience with God.

The Parts of the Picture

The Title. "Quiddity" is a term for the essence of a thing. Although it has other meanings (such as over-subtlety in argument, or quirk, or quibble), perhaps the best way of interpreting the term here is to say that Herbert uses it to indicate that he is dealing with the essence of poetry.

Stanza 1. A listing of things which poetry is not.

Stanza 2. A listing of things poetry cannot do. In line 8 demesne means a domain or land connected to a manor.

Stanza 3. The first two lines of this stanza mention other things which poetry is not, and then in the last two lines the speaker defines poetry as "that which while I use I am with thee." The "use "of poetry for Herbert is experiencing God, and therefore, it is the "Most," the superlative that takes or supersedes all else. Some scholars, however, suggest this phrase is to be interpreted as a proverbial expression meaning "God the all powerful takes complete possession of him"[99] or "While I am with thee, then I most take all."[100]

The Parts of the Picture Come Together

The three stanzas move toward a clarification of what poetry is. The first movement is to point out what poetry is not. The first stanza lists prominent possessions, noteworthy accomplishments, and other items that poetry is not. The second stanza indicates what poetry cannot do (lines 5 and 7-8) and that it has never traveled in France or Spain, the most prestigious of European countries (line 6). Then the essence of poetry for the speaker is stated: "that which while I use/ I am with thee." The definition is not technical but experiential.

When the poet says that poetry is "that which while I use [italics mine] I am with thee," does "use" mean "read" poetry or "write" it, or both? Probably both, but the poet is not concerned with clarifying that issue. What he does make clear is that the experience of poetry (whether reading or writing it) is for him an experience with God. Hence, as John Wall, Jr., aptly explains, "Since through verse, the speaker is with God, poetry thus is seen to excel all other goods or human activities."[101]

Reflections

1. What does the poem have to say about relationship with God?
2. What spiritual direction does it provide?
3. Do you have, as Herbert did with poetry, something that is done solely or primarily to be with God, something you do that is truly God-centered, that is done with the sole, or at least primary, motivation of experiencing God?
4. What is the value of an experience of God? What can it give us that nothing else can?
5. What are the things in ourselves, our lives, and our secular culture that distract us from being devoted to the experience that is solely or primarily for God, to God, and with God?
6. Is the idea of Herbert's experiencing God in poetry similar to the following statement made by Eric Liddell in *Chariots of Fire*: "God made me fast, and when I run, I feel His pleasure."?

Scriptures for further reflection:

Psalm 23:4
Psalm 34:8
Psalm 119:103

THE HOLY SCRIPTURES I

Oh Book! infinite sweetness! let my heart
    Suck every letter, and a honey gain,
    Precious for any grief in any part;
To clear the breast, to mollify all pain.
Thou art all health, health thriving till it make   5
    A full eternity: thou art a mass
    Of strange delights, where we may wish and take.
Ladies, look here; this is the thankful glass,
That mends the looker's eyes: this is the well
    That washes what it shows. Who can endear   10
    Thy praise too much? thou art heaven's Lidger here,
Working against the states of death and hell.
    Thou art joy's handsel: heaven lies flat in thee,
    Subject to every mounter's bended knee.

The Big Picture

What does the Bible mean to you? Dealing with that question has led to conflict and division among Christians, but for many the experience of Scripture is pure joy. In this poem, Scripture is pure joy. The speaker uses a series of images to describe various aspects of his love of Scripture. The images reflect the riches he finds.

The Parts of the Picture

The poem catalogues the delights of Scripture:

- Scripture is "infinite sweetness," and the speaker's heart is to "suck ev'ry letter" in it to gain honey.
- It is "precious for any grief"; it clears the breast (perhaps the heart), and it alleviates pain.
- It is "all health," a health that not only thrives but also produces a "full eternity," with its message of eternal life.
- It is a "mass of strange delights," available for the taking.
- It is the "thankful glass" or a mirror that deserves our gratitude since it mends the eyes of those who look into it.
- It is a "well that washes" or cleanses what it reveals.
- It is praiseworthy.

- It is "heaven's Lidger" (or ambassador on earth), fighting death and hell.
- It is "joy's handsel," or the first installment of the joy that is to follow.
- It has heaven lying flat in it, "subject to" or available to "every mounter's bended knee," an image of one who desires to "mount" upward to heaven but only on a humble and reverent bended knee.

The Parts of the Picture Come Together

Rather than building to a climax, the poem starts on a mountain top and stays there. Rather than ordering the delights of Scripture with any sense of priority, the speaker displays the delights of Scripture with equal joy. Scripture is nourishing and sweet. It is useful in alleviating grief and pain. Its giving of health has an eternal dimension. Its delights are for the taking. It mends and cleanses. It is active in fighting death and hell. It is the first taste of the heavenly joy to come. It has heaven lying flat in it, accessible to the one who approaches humbly on bended knee.

Reflections

1. What does the poem have to say about relationship with God?
2. What spiritual direction does it provide?
3. How would you describe the meaning of the Scriptures for you?
4. To what extent would you agree or disagree with this poem? What would you add to or delete from, or how would you otherwise amend, the descriptions found in the poem?

Scriptures for further reflection:

Romans 15:4
II Timothy 3:16-17
Hebrews 4:12

BIBLIOGRAPHY
of Works Cited

Saint Augustine. *Confessions.* (translated by R. S. Pine-Coffin). New York: Penguin Books, 1961.

Bloom, Harold. *The Best Poems of the English Language.* New York: Harper Collins Publishers. 2007.

Charles, Amy M. *A Life of George Herbert.* Ithaca, N. Y.: Cornell University Press. 1977.

Chute, Marchette. *Two Gentle Men.* New York: E.P. Dutton, Co. 1959.

Eliot, T.S. *George Herbert.* Longmans, Green, and Co. 1968.

Freer, Coburn. *Music for a King.* Baltimore: The Johns Hopkins Press. 1972.

Grant, Patrick. *The Transformation of Sin.* Amherst, Massachusetts: The University of Massachusetts Press. 1974.

Greenwood, E.B. "George Herbert's Sonnet 'Prayer': A Stylistic Study." *Essays in Criticism,* XV (1965), 27-45, as it appears in Mario A. Di. Cesare (ed), *George Herbert and the Seventeenth Century Religious Poets.* New York: W.W. Norton and Co., 1978, pp. 249-55.

Hodgkins, Christopher. *"George Herbert, The Temple." Invitation to the Classics.* Grand Rapids, Michigan: Baker Books. 1998, pp. 159-62.

Hutchinson, F.E. *The Works of George Herbert.* Oxford: Clarendon Press. 1978.

Martz, Louis L. *The Poetry of Meditation.* New Haven: Yale University Press. 1962.

Martz, Louis L., ed. *The Oxford Poetry Library: George Herbert.* New York: Oxford University Press. 1994.

Mursell, Gordon. *English Spirituality.* Louisville, Ky.: Westminster John Knox Press. 2001. Vol. 1.

Norris, Kathleen. "Mercy Me," *Christian Century,* November 29, 2005, p. 20.

Peterson, Eugene H. *Eat This Book.* Grand Rapids, Michigan: William B. Eerdmans. 2006.

Peterson, Eugene H. *Take and Read*. Grand Rapids, Michigan: William B. Eerdmans Publishing Co. 1996.

Piret, Michael. "Herbert and Proverbs," *The Cambridge Quarterly*, 17 (1988).

Roberts, John R., "Me Thoughts I Heard One Calling Child!: Herbert's 'The Collar'"; *Renascense*; Spring, 1993; Vol. 45; Issue 3.

Ryley, George. *Mr. Herbert's Temple and Church Militant Explained and Improved* (Edited by Maureen Boyd and Cedric C. Brown). New York: Garland Publishing, Inc. 1987.

Summers, Joseph H. *George Herbert: His Religion and Art*. Cambridge: Harvard University Press. 1968.

Strier, Richard. *Love Known*. Chicago: The University of Chicago Press. 1983.

Tobin, John (ed.). *George Herbert: The Compete English Poems*. London: Penguin Group. 1991.

Unrau, J. "Three Notes on George Herbert," *N&Q*, 15 (March 1968), pp. 94-95.

Vendler, Helen. *The Poetry of George Herbert*. Cambridge: Harvard University Press. 1975.

Wall, John N. *Transformation of the Word*. Athens, Georgia: The University of Georgia Press. 1988.

Wall, John N., Jr. ed., *George Herbert: The Country Parson, The Temple*. New York: Paulist Press. 1981.

Walton, Izaak. *The Life of Mr. George Herbert* (in Tobin, George Herbert) London: Penguin Group. 1991, pp. 265-314.

White, Helen C. *The Metaphysical Poets*. New York: Collier Books. 1966.

Wilcox, Helen. *The English Poems of George Herbert*. Cambridge: Cambridge University Press, 2007

Wilson, F.P. "A Note on George Herbert's 'The Quidditee," *RES*, 19 (1943), pp. 398-99)

NOTES

[1] Summers, 29-30.

[2] See quotation of Barnabas Oley in Chute, p. 130.

[3] Walton (as contained in Tobin), p. 311.

[4] Hodgkins, p. 159.

[5] Mursell, p. 424.

[6] Bloom, p. 183.

[7] Peterson, *Eat This Book*, pp. 20-21.

[8] Peterson, *Take and Read*, p. 1-2.

[9] Summers, p. 11.

[10] Eliot, p. 24.

[11] Baxter as quoted in Summers, p. 16.

[12] Eliot, p. 21.

[13] Eliot, p. 22.

[14] Charles, p. 199.

[15] Charles, p. 78.

[16] White, p. 173.

[17] Summers, p. 107.

[18] Hutchinson, p. 535.

[19] Wilcox, p. 570.

[20] Tobin, p. 403.

[21] Hutchinson, p. 535.

[22] Charles, pp. 127-28.

[23] Charles, pp. 84-87.

[24] Hutchinson, p. 491.

[25] Wall, p. 241.

[26] Freer, p. 216.

[27] Hutchinson, p. 492.

[28] Wall, p. 245.

[29] Martz, *The Oxford Poetry Library*, p. 198.

[30] Strier, p. 72.

[31] Freer, p. 172.

[32] Strier, p. 92.

[33] Strier pp. 31-32.

[34] Hutchinson, p. 504.

[35] Grant, pp. 124-25.

[36] Strier, pp. 57-58.

[37] Strier, p. 58.

[38] Summers, p. 89.

[39] Martz, *The Oxford Poetry Library*, p. 208.

[40] Ryley, p. 226.

[41] Wall, Jr., ed., *George Herbert*, p. 197.

[42] Wilcox, p. 436.

[43] Summers, p. 144.

[44] Freer, p. 123.

[45] Summers, p. 118.

[46] Hutchinson, p. 541.

[47] Hutchinson, p. 541.

[48] Martz, *The Poetry of Meditation*, p. 61.

[49] Hutchinson, p. 532.

[50] Hutchinson, p. 534.

[51] Wilcox, p. 536.

[52] Tobin, p. 377.

[53] Summers, p. 128.

[54] Hutchinson, p. 533.

[55] Hutchinson, p. 502.

[56] Hutchinson, p. 502.

[57] Wall, *Transformations of the Word*, p. 251.

[58] Bloom, pp. 184-85.

[59] Summers, p. 182.

[60] Hutchinson, p. 493.

[61] Greenwood, p. 250.

[62] Greenwood, p. 250.

[63] Hutchinson, p. 493.

[64] Tobin, p. 347.

[65] Tobin, p. 347-48.

[66] Tobin, p. 348.

[67] Greenwood, p. 253.

[68] Martz, *The Oxford Poetry Library*, p. 179.

[69] Greenwood, p. 255.

[70] Unrau, pp. 94-95 as quoted in Tobin, p. 356.

[71] Hutchinson, p. 540.

[72] Hutchinson, p. 540.

[73] Charles, pp. 163-64.

[74] Charles, pp. 42-43, 51, and 163-64; and Chute, pp.28 and 115.

[75] Chute, p. 115.

[76] Wilcox, p. 236.

[77] Wilcox, p. 236.

[78] Summers, p. 132.

[79] Summers, p. 134.

[80] Summers, p. 132-33.

[81] Summers, p. 133-35.

[82] Norris, p. 20.

[83] Strier, p. 220.

[84] Hutchinson, p. 531; Tobin, p. 397; Wall, Jr. ed., *George Herbert*, p. 278, and Roberts.

[85] Tobin, p. 397.

[86] Wilcox, p. 528.

[87] Summers, p. 90.

[88] Hutchinson, p. 510.

[89] Augustine, p. 21.

[90] Vendler, p. 36.

[91] Vendler, p. 32.

[92] Tobin, p. 395.

[93] Hutchinson, p. 528.

[94] Strier, p. 180.

[95] Freer, p. 121.

[96] Strier, p. 148.

[97] Strier, p. 149.

[98] Strier, p. 149-50.

[99] Wilson, pp. 398-99, as quoted in Tobin, p. 359.

[100] Piret, p. 228, as quoted in Tobin, p. 359.

[101] Wall, in *George Herbert*, p. 186.

WORDS OF THANKSGIVING

*T*hanksgiving, of course, begins with George Herbert. It is with his poetry that this work is solely concerned, and I pray that the sole effect for the reader is the experience of his poetry. For me, however, Herbert's legacy includes but goes beyond his poetry. It extends to the way in which Herbert, in the words of an early biographer, "lost himself in a humble way" in his work with the people of his small parish at Bemerton. Furthermore, and most importantly for me, Herbert's God-centeredness overshadows all else in his poetry and in his life. Sometimes there was the joy of knowing God's love and grace. At other times there was the despairing that accompanies the experience of separation from God. At times there was petition; sometimes there was fulfillment; and at other times, frustration—all involving God. There always seemed to be a problem to work through with God, at times ending in peace, at other times in surrender, and still at other times in uncertainty. But God was always at the center. His poetry was about God, for God, to God, seeking God, celebrating God, working it out with God. Although he prepared his poetry for possible publication at the end of his life, there was nothing in his life or in his poetry that indicated a primary need for acceptance by a literary audience. He had his audience with God and, although publication was indeed a possibility, Herbert's calling came from God and his fulfillment was consummated in God. And so he died in peace (according to the witnesses), not knowing what would become of his poetry, but knowing his God with certainty. Thanks be to God.

And there are others for whom I give thanks. As reflected in the notes throughout this book, I have benefitted greatly from the secondary literature concerning George Herbert, especially the work of Joseph Summers, F. E. Hutchison, Richard Strier, Amy Charles, Louis Martz, and most recently and completely, Helen Wilcox in her definitive modern edition of Herbert's English poems. I am also indebted to special people who were most graciously helpful. I would like to express my deepest gratitude, first, to Dr. Bryan Gillespie, retired professor of English at Stetson University, who has been a treasured friend for many years. He introduced me to Herbert and encouraged and enlightened me along the way with his reading of Herbert. Also, Dr. Clement Goode, retired distinguished professor of English at Baylor University, brought out my love of literature with his brilliance in the classroom when I was his student. He has offered invaluable suggestions on parts of the manuscript. Most importantly, I am indebted, as usual, to my indescribably wonderful wife, Cynthia, who, along with the grace of God, enabled everything.

This book would not have had a beginning and certainly it would not have been completed without the assistance of the secondary literature and the people mentioned above. Whatever is good in this work can be traced back to them in some way. To the extent, however, that errors or other wayward wanderings are found, they are my sole responsibility.

Joseph L. Womack

I am deeply grateful that Mr. Womack has permitted Everyday Education to bring *Working it Out* back into print. It is a wonderful resource for both devotional and learning purposes, and I hope you enjoy it as much as I have.

Janice Campbell
Everyday Education, LLC
2014

Deo gratias.

Lightning Source UK Ltd.
Milton Keynes UK
UKHW01f1845070618
323909UK00001B/250/P